MW00906215

YANKEES
WORLD SERIES MEMORIES

YANKEES
WORLD SERIES MEMORIES

Maury Allen
with Bruce Markusen

SPORTS
PUBLISHING

Sports Publishing books may be purchased in bulk at special
discounts for sales promotion, corporate gifts, fund-raising, or
educational purposes. Special editions can also be created to
specifications. For details, contact the Special Sales Department,
Sports Publishing, 307 West 36th Street, 11th Floor, New York,
NY 10018 or sportspubbooks@skyhorsepublishing.com.

Sports Publishing° is a registered trademark of Skyhorse
Publishing, Inc.°, a Delaware corporation.

Visit our website at www.sportspubbooks.com

10 9 8 7 6 5 4 3 2 1

Library of Congress Cataloging-in-Publication Data is available
on file.

ISBN: 978-1-61321-095-6

Printed in the United States of America

For Amanda, Matt, Ben, and Nina—The Big Four

Contents

Introduction

In 1894, Pittsburgh Pirates owner William C. Temple pushed for a championship series for the two top teams in his National League. The second-place New York Giants swept the first-place Baltimore Orioles in a seven-game series to capture the Temple Cup. The upstart American League got into the act in 1901 and two years later, in 1903, the Boston Americans (no Curse of the Bambino yet) defeated the Pittsburgh Pirates of Honus Wagner five games to three for the "Championship of the United States," soon to be renamed the World Series for no known reason. Every year since the World Series has been played, except for 1904 as a result of National League arrogance and 1994 due to a labor dispute.

In 1921, the once-downtrodden New York Highlanders, escapees from Baltimore, played in their first Series as the Yankees against their Polo Grounds landlords, the New York Giants. The Giants won five games to three. (It was the final time the World Series would experiment with a best-of-nine series format.) John McGraw's Giants came back again to defeat the Yankees in a 1922 Series sweep four games to none. Yet it took the Giants *five* games to do so, as Game 2 ended in a 10-

inning, 3-3 tie as the sun went down. Yankees right fielder Babe Ruth had only two hits in the series.

Yankee Stadium, the House That Ruth Built and Steinbrenner is building anew, opened the following year. So began the Yankees' World Series dominance with a victory over the hated Giants, four games to two. From that day—October 15, 1923—until now, the New York Yankees have been the most successful team in the history of sports with 26 titles in 39 Fall Classic appearances. Not even the absence of a World Series appearance since 2003 or the inability to gain a World Series championship ring since 2000 can challenge the team's domination.

As a youngster growing up in New York—mad about baseball and determined to play the game for a living, or at least write about it after curve balls and ground balls ended my athletic dreams—I measured time by World Series games. A new year began with the Fall Classic. I saw my first World Series game in person as a teenager in 1947, the Brooklyn Dodgers against the New York Yankees, Game 3 of the Series, a vivid memory that remains 60 years later. My brother and I slept overnight on the sidewalk outside Brooklyn's Ebbets Field waiting for the gates to open at 10 a.m. so we could purchase our $1.10 bleacher seats. That day at the ballpark, we ate our salami sandwiches, chewed on a candy bar, and sipped soda as we watched Joe DiMaggio, Tommy Henrich, Phil Rizzuto, and Snuffy Stirnweiss take batting practice. No matter that the Yankees lost that Series game 9-8. I sat thrilled and breathless for the entire game. We stood later in the Ebbets Field rotunda as players exited the stadium, screaming their names as they briskly passed on their way to the waiting team bus. "Joe, Joe," I shouted as DiMaggio passed, walking lightly on the rotunda floor, wearing a long dark overcoat with his slick, black hair almost shining in the late afternoon sunlight. The Yankees won that thriller of a Series four games to three.

They missed out in 1948 as I watched the Cleveland Indians beat the Boston Braves on the small television set in my neighbor's home. Then in October of 1949, the Yankees began the most astonishing streak in baseball history, never matched in almost six decades: five straight championships in five years under the direction of manager Casey Stengel. The World Series seemed to become the personal property of the Yankees throughout the 1950s with eight appearances in ten seasons between 1950 and 1959. They only missed the October fun in 1954 and 1959, beaten out twice by manager Al Lopez with the Cleveland Indians in 1954 and again with the Chicago White Sox in 1959.

Five more appearances in the Fall Classic from 1960 through 1964, now witnessed in person as a working sportswriter, added to the Yankees' lore and lustre.

In the late 1960s and early 1970s, the team slowed down considerably under CBS ownership. Then Billy Martin brought the Yankees back to the Series in 1976. Two more championships followed in 1977 and 1978 under the rambunctious leadership of Martin and strong-willed team owner George Steinbrenner. The Yankees were in the Series again in 1981, then slipped into another prolonged absence until the arrival of Joe Torre as field boss in 1996. There were six Yankee appearances in the World Series in the first eight years of Torre's time as skipper.

Over the last 60 years I have witnessed every Yankee World Series game as a fan, a working newspaper sportswriter, or a baseball author. I have collected the thrills and the disappointments in my memory bank. With ease, I can recall Don Larsen striking out Dale Mitchell for his perfect game in 1956, and Yogi Berra drifting back slowly to the left-field wall as Bill Mazeroski's fly ball sailed over his head for the game-winning home run in Game 7 of the 1960 Classic. There's Bernie Williams camping under a Mike Piazza drive to center field to record the last out of the 2000 Series when the Yankees and New York Mets played for the first time in the modern version of the Subway Series. In the following pages, I have exhausted my memory in replaying so many of the Yankees Series triumphs and tragedies. Beginning with my first Yankee October in 1947 and moving through the most recent appearances. In my mind, I have rated each appearance on the merits of excitement, drama, heroics, and history. Now, in order, come the tales of my favorite Yankee World Series.

–Maury Allen

YANKEES
WORLD SERIES MEMORIES

1

1947

The 1947 World Series wasn't short on memorable occasions: a near no-hitter pitched by journeyman Yankee hurler Bill Bevens, who won only seven games in the entire 1947 season; a clutch ninth-inning, pinch-hit double off the wall in Ebbets Field by retiring Brooklyn infielder Harry "Cookie" Lavagetto that not only broke up the near no-hitter but won the game for the Dodgers; a miraculous catch in the sixth game at Yankee Stadium by diminutive outfielder Al Gionfriddo; probably the finest relief pitching performance in World Series history turned in by lefthander Joe Page, who logged five scoreless innings of one-hit ball to wrap up Game 7 for the Yankees.

Then there was modern baseball's first African-American player, Jackie Robinson, who played first base in all seven games, batted .259, showed his electrifying skills on the bases, and opened the door for an integrated baseball future. Robinson, of course, would go on to a Hall of Fame career as a second baseman and later third baseman and outfielder for the Brooklyn Dodgers.

To catch a glimpse of the action on October 2, 1947, I had to spend a long, thrilling night on the Bedford Avenue sidewalk waiting for the gates to open at 10 a.m. A brown bag with two salami sandwiches, a candy bar, and an apple were in hand as I boarded the BMT Express from the Kings Highway stop in Brooklyn to the Prospect Avenue stop late that in the afternoon. I walked the three blocks to the ballpark with my older brother, settled on the ground with the lunch bag and the Brooklyn Eagle newspaper, and waited for the greatest thrill of my young life, a World Series ticket for a bleacher seat.

For the drama of that brilliantly played seven-game series, for the historic appearance of Jackie Robinson, and for the lasting memory of witnessing a World Series game in person for the very first time, I consider the 1947 Series between the Yankees and the Brooklyn Dodgers my personal Series favorite.

I'll let Ralph Branca set the scene:

"I remember it like it was yesterday," said Branca, the 21-year-old Brooklyn starter in Game 1. "My brother Julius drove me down to Yankee Stadium from our home in nearby Mount Vernon. I didn't say much in the car. I was just thinking of those Yankee hitters: (Tommy) Henrich; (Joe) DiMaggio; Yogi Berra, the good rookie lefthanded hitter; George McQuinn, the tough first baseman; and the slugging outfielder Johnny Lindell."

Branca was sitting on the back porch of the 19th hole of the Otesaga Hotel golf course in Cooperstown, New York as he recalled his emotions from that day nearly 60 years ago.

"I had a great year and felt pretty confident facing those famous Yankees. We had a wonderful ball club and I was sure I could handle them. I certainly did for the first four innings. Then DiMaggio hit that infield single and I went to pieces," recalled Branca.

Bad nerves attacked the youngster, who walked McQuinn, hit Billy Johnson with a pitch, gave up a double to Lindell, and walked Phil Rizzuto before being relieved. By inning's end, the

Yankees had scored five runs on their way to an opening-game 5-3 triumph.

"I know I lost my poise in that fifth inning," Branca remembered, "but I couldn't understand then and can't understand to this day why I didn't get a chance to start another game. After all, I had anchored our staff all year and got us there."

The 80-year-old Branca, later to gain even more immortal baseball fame in 1951 after the famous Shot Heard 'Round the World by Bobby Thomson of the New York Giants, grits his teeth when he talks of the 1947 Brooklyn manager.

"Burt Shotton took over after Leo Durocher was suspended at the start of the 1947 season, and despite my pitching all year he just forgot me in the Series. That always hurt. I thought things might have been different if I started another game," Branca said.

The Yankees coasted to a 10-3 win in the second game behind Allie Reynolds, and the Series shifted to Brooklyn's Ebbets Field for the third game, my first World Series game. The Dodgers won a slugfest 9-8. More importantly, I ate about half a dozen ballpark franks, downed six or seven sodas, and saved my scorecard from the game, which I still have today.

Brooklyn tied the Series at two games each in Game 4, one of the most historic games in the sport's history. Bevens, a 6-foot-4, 220-pound right-hander from Hubbard, Oregon, who would have only a four-year big league career, was 7-13 that season for Yankee manager Bucky Harris.

He walked ten Dodgers in that game; gave up a single run in the fifth on two walks, a sacrifice, and an infield out; and carried a no-hitter into the ninth inning. In the final frame with the Yankees ahead 2-1, Bevens walked Carl Furillo with one out and then retired rookie third baseman Johnny Jorgensen on a foul ball for the second out. Shotton then made a strange move, which Harris countered with an even stranger one.

The Brooklyn skipper, who always wore street clothes in the dugout, sent in the veteran outfielder Gionfriddo to run for Furillo. On the second pitch Gionfriddo stole second base to put the tying run on second. Shotton sent injured slugger Pete Reiser out of the lineup with a damaged foot, up to bat for reliever Hugh Casey.

In one of the most controversial moves in World Series history, Harris went against the book and walked Reiser, the potential winning run, intentionally. It was the tenth walk of the game for Bevens. Infielder Eddie Miksis ran for the limping Reiser. Then came up another pinch hitter, veteran Harry (Cookie) Lavagetto, a right-handed line-drive hitter in his final big league season. Lavagetto, hitting for Brooklyn second baseman Eddie Stanky, stood between Bevens and a no-hitter. He lined Bevens' second pitch past right fielder Tommy Henrich off the wall in right. Gionfriddo scored easily from second, and Miksis, with great speed, slid home safely with the winning run on a great charge from first.

"I thought about that hit for years," Bevens once said. "I tried to get the pitch high and away from Lavagetto. I guess it wasn't high enough and far enough away."

"Sometimes you don't always get a pitch where you want it," said Berra, then a rookie catcher.

The 3-2 Brooklyn victory tied the Series at two games each, setting up an exciting Series finish. In the fifth game, DiMaggio homered off fireballer Rex Barney in the top of the fifth inning, and Frank "Spec" Shea, who won 14 games as a rookie during the regular season, picked up his second Series triumph by allowing just four hits and one run in nine innings.

The Yankees took a 3-2 Series lead into Game 6, one of the most thrilling contests in World Series history. The Dodgers were trailing 5-4 heading into the sixth inning. They rallied against reliever Joe Page in the top of the sixth with the key hit an RBI pinch-hit double by third-string catcher Bobby Bragan. It was amazing that Bragan was still on the Dodgers roster in the Fall Classic. He was from Birmingham, Alabama, and was one of the leaders of a petition that spring, along with southerners Dixie Walker and Eddie Stanky and misguided Pennsylvanian Carl Furillo, that implored the Dodgers to refrain from bringing

African-American player Jackie Robinson to Brooklyn.

"I said I wanted to be traded but Mr. (Branch) Rickey, the Brooklyn boss, asked us to hold off until we saw this guy play. It wasn't long before I appreciated his play and saw what a wonderful man Jackie was. We soon became very close friends," Bragan said.

In that sixth game, Bragan was summoned out of the bullpen with the Dodgers down by a run to hit for Branca, who had made his second relief appearance in the series after starting the opener.

"I was nervous when I was walking to the bat rack, but as I got closer to the plate I grew more calm," Bragan said. "I felt good that Page was left handed and that might help. He hung a curve and I drove it down the line for a run-scoring double. Pee Wee Reese got a two-run-scoring single and suddenly we had an 8-5 lead."

Shotton sent Gionfriddo, all of 5-foot-6, to the Brooklyn outfield in the bottom of the sixth to replace Miksis, an infielder by trade who got into the game as a pinch hitter for left fielder Gene Hermanski and played one inning in the outfield. Now the Yankees, trying to close out the Series in six games, rallied again against left-hander Joe Hatten. They got a couple of runners on with DiMaggio at bat. The Yankee Clipper caught one of Hatten's high fastballs and drove it to the deepest part of left-center field in Yankee Stadium. The left-handed-throwing Gionfriddo, with the glove on his right hand, raced back and to his right for the huge drive. He lost his cap near the rail, reached up, and snatched the baseball out of the air as he crashed into the low railing of the visiting team's bullpen.

"I was back in the bullpen warming up pitchers again by then so I probably had the best view of the catch," said Bragan. "Frankly, with Al's small size, I never thought he had a chance to catch it. Somehow he stretched out as far as he could and grabbed the ball just before it disappeared into the bullpen for a game-tying homer."

Gionfriddo has always recognized the catch as the highlight

of his short big-league career over four seasons in Pittsburgh and Brooklyn.

"It was not only an amazing catch," Gionfriddo once said, "but it was against the great DiMaggio. I think that is why it is as well remembered by fans today as it was in those old days."

DiMaggio has always found the catch about as annoying a baseball experience as the Yankee Clipper ever had. The catch, which is often replayed during modern World Series games, caused the reserved DiMaggio to kick some dirt around second base after Gionfriddo gloved his 415-foot drive.

Hatten and reliever Hugh Casey shut the Yankees down the rest of the way for an 8-6 Brooklyn win, which tied the dramatic Series at three games each. Shea got the nod for his third start of the Series, this time against right-hander Hal Gregg. He lasted just an inning and a third, and the Dodgers led 2-1 into the fourth. Then the best pinch hitter the Yankees had, Bobby Brown, who later became president of the American League, tied it up with a double. The Yankees went ahead that same inning on the clutch hitting of Tommy Henrich, the famed "Old Reliable" of the Yankees, who smacked a single off Brooklyn reliever Hank Behrman.

Harris brought in Page as soon as the Yankees moved ahead in the game, and DiMaggio's pitching pal settled the Series with five scoreless innings. Only a ninth-inning single by Miksis marred Page's perfect pitching as the Yankees moved ahead for the 5-2 victory before 74,065 fans at the Stadium.

"He only had one good pitch, a fastball, but it really moved," remembered Berra. "If he had his control nobody could touch him. He was that good in the final game and I knew we had it won."

The Series victory gave the Yankees their 11th victory in 25 years and their second over Brooklyn in seven years. It was the start of an agonizing October trend for the Dodgers that lasted until they finally won one over the Yankees in the 1955 World Series.

For me, it was the start of watching some six decades of

Series play in person or on the television screen. The memories of Lavagetto getting that hit off Bevens, Gionfriddo catching Joe D's drive, Page shutting down the Dodgers in the seventh game, and that rookie Dodger, Robinson, running wild, make the 1947 Series the most thrilling I can remember.

Try to catch a better Series over the next 24 trips in Yankee Series lore.

2

1960

The 1960 World Series was a wild and crazy scene: the Pittsburgh Pirates set to play against the Yankees for the first time since the famed Murderers' Row sweep in 1927. On the field, the Yankees rattled the walls at the Stadium and Forbes Field for 91 hits and 55 runs, yet still lost four games to three. Bill Mazeroski, a .273 hitter with 11 homers during the season, smacked two homers, including the first walk-off, Series-ending home run in history. Yankee shortstop Tony Kubek was hit in the throat by a routine ground ball off the bat of Bill Virdon after the grounder hit a pebble. Mickey Mantle, seeing Kubek later bleeding in the training room, was brought to tears.

Manager Casey Stengel, handling his last World Series for the Yankees after seven championships and ten pennants in 12 Yankee seasons, made the daring move of starting journeyman right hander Art Ditmar twice, including the opener; both wound up losses for New York. Ralph Terry lost one game for New York as a starter and another in relief; Pittsburgh reliever Harvey Haddix did the opposite, winning the seventh game in relief after taking the fifth game as a starter. Yankee second baseman Bobby Richardson collected 11 hits and 12 RBIs on the way to the Series MVP award, but it was Mazeroski's dramatic home run over left fielder Yogi Berra's head that was celebrated around the country. That blast was even more memorable for me because I was there for the first time as a working sportswriter. I covered the first game of my 40 World Series on October 5, 1960, at Forbes Field.

The night before the first Series game, all of the New York City sportswriters gathered together for a dinner hosted by Bob Fishel, the legendary public relations director of the Yankees, in a downtown Pittsburgh restaurant. Fishel had worked for rambunctious St. Louis Browns owner Bill Veeck and steered Veeck's famous midget pinch hitter, Eddie Gaedel, wearing Browns uniform number 1/8, to his memorable at-bat. Fishel's skill, on this Pittsburgh night, was simply picking up the check. After the dinner a few of the sportswriters walked to a nearby Pittsburgh nightspot. Writer and television personality Dick Schaap led a small group to a back table for a performance by comedian Lenny Bruce. Bruce had gained immense notoriety by using obscenities freely in his comedy act, which would later lead to legal turmoil for the freewheeling entertainer.

Bruce finished his act to much applause and great laughter and soon joined the table of sportswriters. Schaap had known him for some time.

"I'm a great Yankee fan and this is a terrific thrill for me," Bruce told us. "It's also a thrill to be with you guys. When I was a kid I thought I might become a sportswriter."

The only other time I could recall a celebrity claiming he really would have preferred becoming a sportswriter occurred in 1969 during a White House reception during the Washington, D.C., All-Star game. President Richard Nixon, then bogged down in the histrionics of the Vietnam war, recited the starting lineup of his favorite team, the Chicago White Sox in the late 1930s, before suggesting his real role in life was to be as a sportswriter.

"I wish you had realized your dream," I told the president later, in my own opposition to the war, as we moved quickly through a presidential reception line.

Bruce sat with the group for nearly half an hour before his next show. He never uttered a bad word and promised he would come to a game if his schedule permitted.

Back at Forbes, Stengel sent Ditmar out to the mound for the opener amidst media controversy, and Ditmar proved the media right. With one out in the first inning, he was yanked from the game before he could break a sweat after surrendering three runs. That came after Roger Maris, who would make baseball history the next season with 61 homers in 1961 (the greatest single baseball feat in the history of the game in my opinion), slugged a homer for a 1-0 Yankee lead for Ditmar in the top of the first. Jim Coates, a hard-throwing right hander known as a head hunter, was touched for two more runs in relief of Ditmar. Meanwhile, Pirates starter Vern Law and reliever Roy Face, a fork ball specialist who had an 18-1 record in 1959, shut the Yankees down for a 6-4 victory, made close only by a ninth inning pinch hit two run homer by Elston Howard.

Stengel, who led the league in grouchiness following tough losses, was asked after the game to justify giving 15-game winner Ditmar the start over future Hall of Famer Whitey Ford.

"Because I wanted to," the manager replied.

The Yankees began their slugging onslaught in the second game when they posted a 16-3 victory. Mickey Mantle smashed two huge home runs, one of them traveling a measured 478 feet over the wall in the deepest part of Forbes' right-center field. The center field area was so vast at Forbes that the pregame batting cage remained on the field during games, nestled against the wall more than 500 feet away from home plate because there was so little possibility of anyone hitting a ball that far.

The Yankees won the third game 10-0 behind the pitching

of Ford, who finally got a Series start in Yankee Stadium. Richardson had six RBIs with a grand-slam homer and a two-run single on his way to a record-breaking 12 RBIs for the Series. That was quite a feat for the second baseman, who had mustered just 26 RBIs in 150 games during the 1960 regular season.

"I just got hot that week. It's hard to explain," Richardson later said. "Every pitch to me just seemed as big as a basketball. I swung hard and just connected almost every time up."

It earned him the Series MVP to the great disappointment of Mazeroski who was later consoled when enshrined in the Baseball Hall of Fame in 2001.

Law, with relief help again from Face as well as an RBI double of his own off Terry, led the Pirates to a Series-tying, 3-2 victory in Game 4. The Pirates collected only seven hits, but bunched a handful together to score all three runs in the fifth inning.

By now, the Series was taking on an unusual tone with the Pirates winning two well-pitched games and the Yankees winning their two games by a combined 23 runs.

The Pirates went ahead three games to two with a 5-2 victory in the fifth game on the solid pitching of Haddix and Face, who earned his third save of two or more innings in the series. Stengel, as stubborn as a guy could be, brought Ditmar back as a Game 5 starter despite the opening-game fiasco, and again Ditmar failed the Yankees and was lifted in the second inning.

With New York on the cusp of defeat, rumors flew that if the team couldn't rally back to beat the Pirates it would be the swan song for the 70-year-old skipper. Ralph Houk was waiting in the wings at Triple-A Denver to take over the team. Stengel did get fired by the Yankees after the Series ended, and he uttered one of his most memorable lines at his farewell press conference: "I'll never make the mistake of being 70 again."

Game 6 was another Yankees powerhouse performance with 17 hits—including a pair of triples for Richardson—in a 12-0 rout. Ford cruised through nine innings for his second shutout of the series. Stengel angered one of his players with an in-game decision for the second time in the series. The first occasion came in the second inning of Game 1 as Stengel pinch hit for third baseman Clete Boyer. ("I still hate the old guy," Boyer said of Stengel in a 2006 interview.) Stengel, who didn't bother himself with the feelings of his sensitive players, sent in a pinch runner for catcher Elston Howard in the second inning of Game 6. That runner, pitcher Eli Grba, was then replaced by backup catcher John Blanchard, who went on to collect three hits and knock in a run in the Yankee romp. Howard was more forgiving, saying he understood the move: "Casey thought it would help us win."

Now the Series was tied at three games each. The press gathered around Stengel after the winning game for comment. This time he showcased his sense of humor.

"I'm not going to live or die after the game tomorrow," he said about the final game of the Series.

Baseball history is replete with dramatic games, exciting starts and finishes, breathless plays and late-inning heroics. The seventh game of the 1960 World Series on October 13, 1960, had all that in spades. It may well be one of the most stirring games ever played. I admit that I lost all my objectivity as a working sportswriter for the *New York Post*, rooting like crazy for a Yankee win in this wildest of World Series contests.

Bullet Bob Turley was the Yankee starter in the game Stengel knew might settle his managerial fate. Opposing him was Law, making his third start of the series. He was suffering some ankle problems, and Pittsburgh manager Danny Murtaugh notified his bullpen to be ready if he had to get Law out of there early.

Bob Skinner, a slugging outfielder, was back in the Pittsburgh lineup after injuring his thumb in the first game. Murtaugh went with Rocky Nelson at first base instead of the hot dog, Dick Stuart, who crushed 66 home runs in one minor league season well before Maris hit 61 as a Yankee. Stuart marked the event by scribbling the number 66 in his baseball glove and often talked of himself in the third person as "old 66."

The Pirates wasted no time. Skinner walked with two outs in the bottom of the first, and Nelson drove Turley's fastball over the wall in right for a 2-0 lead. In the second inning, Virdon, once a Yankee farmhand and later the team manager, lined a two-run single for a 4-0 Pittsburgh lead. New York finally got on the board in the fifth when Moose Skowron hit a lead-off, solo home run. Law, failing quickly because of ankle pain, gave up a hit to Richardson to begin the sixth, then walked Tony Kubek. Face relieved Law for the fourth time in the series, but this time the Yankees were ready for him. Mantle singled home a run to make it a 4-2 game, and Yogi Berra, who made a career of these things, hit a clutch, three-run homer to give the Yankees a 5-4 lead.

"I thought that would do it," Berra recalled in 2006. "We had a lot of good pitchers to hold the lead."

Face, wearing down now after a heavy series workload, allowed two more runs in the eighth inning as the Yankees built a 7-4 lead. Berra walked, Skowron and Blanchard singled, and Boyer, still angry after his pinch-hitting embarrassment in Game 1, doubled in another run. Just six outs separated the Yankees from their 19th title. What could be easier?

Bobby Shantz, a tiny left-hander, was the Yankee pitcher in the eighth. With five innings pitched already, Shantz gave up a single to Gino Cimoli. That brought up Virdon, the smooth-fielding Pittsburgh center fielder. He hit a hard ground ball to shortstop that was labeled a double play in any scorer's book that day, including mine. The double play would have killed the Pirates off that inning and probably ended their hopes for a Series triumph. But it didn't materialize. The bouncing ball caught a Forbes Field pebble, jumped sharply in the air, crashed into Kubek's throat as he bent down for the baseball, and knocked him to the ground. The ball trickled away for a hit and the Yankees gathered around Kubek, who eventually was helped off the field by trainer Gus Mauch, a towel held tightly around Kubek's bleeding neck.

Dick Groat, the famed All-America basketball player from

Duke and now the Pirates shortstop, followed with another single for a run. Jim Coates replaced Shantz. An infield hit by 25-year-old Roberto Clemente was good for another run to bring the Pirates to within one. That brought Hal Smith, the backup catcher to Smoky Burgess, to the plate. He connected on the biggest hit of his life, a three-run homer off Coates that put the Pirates ahead 9-7. Just like that, the Yankees appeared on the verge of defeat.

Veteran starter Bob Friend, one of the game's smartest pitchers, faced the Yankees in the top of the ninth. Richardson and Dale Long each singled off the right-hander to open the frame. Murtaugh brought in lefty Harvey Haddix to close out the game. Haddix retired the left-handed Maris on a foul fly ball but gave up a run-scoring single to the switch-hitting Mantle, batting from the right side.

The next play was one of the strangest in World Series history. Gil McDougald, running for Long, led off third, and Mantle, in his final years as an effective base runner before injuries would slow him down noticeably, was a few feet off first. Berra smashed a rocket toward first base. First baseman Rocky Nelson, not known for his quickness or his glove, was spun around as he tried to make an inning-double play. He should have thrown the ball to second to force Mantle and then collected the return throw from the shortstop to end the game. Instead, he looked home and saw McDougald a few feet from home plate with the tying run. He didn't throw to second for a force but tagged first base to retire Berra and whirled to tag Mantle as he lunged back toward first base. With the force out now off the table because of the out at first on the grounder, Mantle slid away from Nelson's tag and was ruled safe at first. McDougald scored to tie the game at 9-9. It was a brilliant play by Mickey and, well, a rocky one by Nelson.

Now the Pirates were coming to bat in the bottom of the ninth in a tie game. Mazeroski, the splendid second baseman with the smooth glove, was the leadoff hitter.

"I just thought about hitting the ball hard," recalled

Mazeroski, as he sat in the lounge of the Otesaga Hotel in Cooperstown, New York during the 2006 Hall of Fame induction weekend. "I had no idea about hitting one out. I never thought of that. We had a lot of good hitters on the bench. I knew if I could get on (that) somebody would move me along and then the top of the order would get me home. I just wanted to get a good pitch."

Terry was the Yankees reliever. He threw Mazeroski a curve ball on the first pitch for ball one. Now he wanted a fastball up and in on Mazeroski, hoping it would jam the Pittsburgh second baseman.

"Maybe the pitch was a little more over the plate than Terry wanted," Maz said. "It all happened so fast I wasn't sure. Even after all these years and no matter how many times I see it on television I am still not sure of where it was."

The pitch was out over the plate and letter high. Mazeroski swung hard and the ball sailed out toward the left-field wall. Berra, playing left field while Johnny Blanchard did the catching that day, started back and to his left.

"I didn't think it was really hit that hard when I first saw it off the bat," Berra recalled. "I started back with the idea that if I got to the wall quickly I would catch it before it hit over my head."

Instead, the ball continued to sail, seemingly picking up momentum as Berra drifted back toward the left-field wall. It went the distance and soon cleared the wall as Berra began to curve away from the back fence.

"I saw it clear the wall and all I could think of was, 'There goes my money.' World Series winning shares meant a lot in those days. We didn't make that much money," Berra said.

Mazeroski ran around second as the ball cleared the wall, jogged happily into third base, and headed home as several fans escorted him to home plate. Umpire Bill Jackowski watched Mazeroski touch the plate and then dashed for the Pittsburgh dugout to escape the oncoming rush of delirious fans.

"All I really remember about it was being drenched in the

clubhouse by a lot of happy guys," said Mazeroski.

In the Yankee clubhouse, Mantle walked into the trainer's room. He saw Kubek still lying on the table with that bloody towel held firm around his neck. Mantle burst into tears at the sight. A doctor had not yet arrived to treat the injury and transport Kubek to the hospital. Stengel, the losing manager in a Series for only the third time in his brilliant Yankee career, was being hounded by the press, not about the game but about his own managerial future. When asked whether he thought he was too elderly to manage again in 1961, Stengel shouted, "How do I know? A lot of people my age are dead at the present time."

It had been a thrilling World Series from the opening pitch to Mazeroski's final swing in the late afternoon of October 13, 1960. Mazeroski's dance around third while rounding the bases—his cap in his hand—has been burned into my memory.

"I still have the cap I was wearing somewhere in my home," Mazeroski said. "I held tight to it that day and I hold tight to it this day."

All these years later the memories of the 1960 World Series remain vivid for me, pleasant for any member of the Pirates and just a little bitter for the Yankee members of that team.

3

1962

Ralph Terry, a 6-foot-3 right-hander born in a fork in the road called Big Cabin, Oklahoma, stood on the mound at San Francisco's Candlestick Park during the late afternoon of October 16, 1962. Yankee manager Ralph Houk was on his way to the mound—his team clinging to a 1-0 lead—to speak to his 26-year-old starting pitcher. Matty Alou was on third base representing the tying run for the Giants, and Willie Mays stood on second as the winning run. The man at the plate was left-handed slugger Willie McCovey, who had already homered once in the 1962 World Series.

Mets skipper Casey Stengel once asked pitcher Roger Craig a pertinent question with McCovey at the plate: "Where do you want me to play the outfielders, in the upper deck or the lower deck?"

Walking McCovey to load the bases was one option. But

Orlando Cepeda, known as the Baby Bull for his huge physique and powerful blasts, waited on deck. It would get no easier for Terry. Houk glanced at the open base at first.

"What do you want to do?" Houk asked the ace of his staff.

"I'd just as soon get it over now," Terry replied.

Houk turned from the mound, walked back toward the Yankee dugout, and leaned his right foot on the top step. Terry could be only thinking at this memorable moment of the similar position he was in two years earlier when he faced Pittsburgh's leadoff hitter, Bill Mazeroski, in the bottom of the ninth inning of a tied Game 7. That confrontation ended famously, more so for Mazeroski than Terry.

Terry had won 23 games for the 1962 Yankees. He had lost Game 2 of the '62 Series due to the brilliant pitching of Jack Sanford, and won the fifth game 5-3 with an efficient six-hitter. Now it was the seventh game of this tense series between these rivals, the former New York Giants, who had played across the Harlem River from Yankee Stadium in the Polo Grounds, and the Yankees, led by the famed M and M Boys, Roger Maris and Mickey Mantle, who had combined for 115 homers only the year before in the celebrated home-run season of 1961.

Giants manager Alvin Dark had gotten both his big sluggers, McCovey and Cepeda, into the seventh-game lineup by moving McCovey to left field and playing Cepeda at first base. Now they were ready to win the series for San Francisco.

"It wasn't just winning the Series that mattered for me," said Cepeda, as the Hall of Famer made his annual visit to Cooperstown in 2006. "It was the thrill of playing in it."

Cepeda recalled that as a kid growing up in Ponce, Puerto Rico, he and his father often talked about the great Yankees and Yankee Stadium.

"Then there I was in the third game walking on the field at the famed Yankee Stadium, the home of Ruth and Gehrig and DiMaggio and all those historic Yankees. I just looked out at that huge place and walked on that grass and examined those stands and I simply felt overwhelmed. It was just so thrilling."

By the finale of the '62 Series, the thrill had worn off a bit as Cepeda waited on deck for Terry to make his crucial decision. The right-hander would pitch to the left-handed McCovey no matter what the classic baseball book might say. Dark thought he had the edge for the tie or the win if McCovey delivered; Houk, meanwhile, prepared himself to face the grinding questions of the annoying members of the press about why he had defied tradition. That is, unless Terry came through.

The Yankees had gotten their only run of that seventh game when Skowron scored on a double-play ball in the fifth. Terry had set the Giants down in order through five innings. In the sixth, San Francisco got its first hit of the game when pitcher Jack Sanford singled. In the seventh, McCovey tripled with two outs but was stranded as Cepeda struck out. Now in the bottom of the ninth, Matty Alou, who played in the same outfield that season with his brother, Felipe, led off the ninth with a bunt single. With the lead runner on, Terry struck out Felipe and Chuck Hiller, then allowed a double into the right-field corner off the bat of Willie Mays.

Roger Maris, the Yankee right fielder that day, displayed his fielding adeptness on Mays' double. The ball was headed for the corner as Alou, a fast runner, raced toward third. Maris was playing the right-handed Mays toward center field; raced to his left, picked up the ball on the run, whirled, and fired the ball on a line to cutoff man Bobby Richardson near second base. Alou, realizing he was dead at the plate if he tried to score, skidded on the grass around third base and scurried back to the bag.

With two outs and the World Series on the line, Terry released his first pitch against McCovey. Far from fooled, McCovey smashed the first pitch down the line in right field, but the ball was pulled too hard and crashed into the stands, a long foul ball.

"I thought McCovey was a powerful free swinger that I might be able to fool," Terry said. "I thought if I kept him in the ball park we could get him out."

Following a curve for a ball, McCovey hit Terry's 1-1 fastball on a wicked line toward right field. Richardson, playing the slugger deep and almost on the grass, raised his glove to snag the drive for the final out.

"I really didn't have time to think about it," recalled Richardson. "It was just hit too hard."

Baseball, a famed game of inches, was surely that in the 1962 Series. Whitey Ford won the series opener in San Francisco with a neat 6-2 victory, despite seeing his 33 ⅔ scoreless inning streak in World Series play come to an end. Sanford pitched a sparkling three-hitter to even the series for San Francisco in Game 2. McCovey smashed a solo home run in the seventh to provide extra cushion in the 2-0 Giant win.

The Yankees pulled ahead in the series on the strength of a surprising pitching feat by journeyman Bill Stafford, who allowed the Giants only four hits in pitching a complete game. The Yankees broke up a scoreless duel and scored three runs in the seventh against left-handed starter Billy Pierce and reliever Don Larsen, just three regular seasons removed from pitching for the Yankees. Houk allowed his burr-cut righty, Stafford, to finish the game himself despite a ninth-inning double by Mays and a home run by catcher Ed Bailey that brought the Giants to within one run, 3-2.

In the see-saw Series the Giants tied it up at two games each with a 7-3 victory in Game 4. The big blow was the first grand-slam home run hit by a National Leaguer. Chuck Hiller, the light-hitting second baseman, slugged a line drive into the stands in right for four runs, providing the margin of victory. Larsen, in relief again, picked up the victory with a third of an inning of scoreless pitching—not quite as glamorous as his 1956 perfecto but significant nevertheless.

The Yankees regained the series lead in a 5-3 triumph in Game 5 that was made possible by a three-run homer from rookie left fielder Tom Tresh. Terry went the distance for New York, striking out seven.

Now the teams traveled west again to resume play in California, but old Mother Nature took over the town with three days of drenching rain. The delay—coupled with a New York rainout—pushed the series to 13 days. The Yankee players got so weary of the idleness that Houk bussed the team down the California coast some 60 miles to a college campus for a needed workout.

"The best part of that was the coeds chasing after us for our autographs," said backup infielder Phil Linz.

Away from the field, the Yankees cleaned out a few local bars and visited some impressive restaurants during the break from play. One of the things never taught in journalism school, even for dedicated future sportswriters, is what to write on the day of a rainout. By the third stormy day, our stories became pretty limp. Every writer searched out a California angle, and Willie Mays—a recognized street stickball player while playing for the New York Giants—had to admit he missed the streets of Harlem after five years in San Francisco.

The team was anxious to end the series. They had a rested Whitey Ford, the game's greatest World Series pitcher, ready for the assignment. Unfortunately for the Yankees, he wasn't at the top of his game. San Francisco's Billy Pierce was, however. A 35-year-old left-hander who weighed 160 pounds soaking wet, Pierce didn't throw hard but had great control and knew an awful lot about changing speeds. He had been a 20-game winner for the White Sox in 1957 and was 16-6 for the pennant-winning Giants in 1962. Pierce had been masterful in winning Game 1 of the Giants' three-game playoff with the Dodgers to decide the 1962 NL pennant winner after both teams finished tied in the standings. In that game, he had outpitched Sandy Koufax; now in Game 6, he outdueled another Hall of Famer in Ford with a three-hit gem to lead San Francisco to a 5-2 win. A fourth-inning single by Felipe Alou and a walk to Mays got the Giants started. Ford, usually an excellent fielder, then threw back to second in a pickoff attempt. The ball sailed into center field. Alou scored on the error, Mays hustled to third, and Cepeda followed with a double for a 2-0 lead. The Yankees never recovered. Maris got a run back in the fifth with a homer, but San Francisco got a couple more runs off Ford in their half of the fifth to lock it up.

Terry and Sanford went at each other again in the tense series finale. In the top of the fifth, the Yankees singled twice to open the frame. A walk to Terry loaded the bases with no outs, and Skowron scored from third on Kubek's double-play grounder to tally the lone run of the game. Terry seemed to strengthen on the mound as the game progressed, never once considering that he could lose again in the seventh game as he had two years earlier in Pittsburgh.

"The secret of big league pitching is that each start is separate and unique. You may have your stuff or you may not. Each game is different and you really don't carry the burden of any other game into the contest. It was only after the game was over and the writers began asking about my memories of the Mazeroski homer that I even thought of his name," Terry said years later.

The tall, handsome right-hander, who later became a successful golf professional with a fluid swing, got out of one tough jam in the bottom of the ninth to preserve the Yankees' 20th Series flag. The victory marked a turning point for New York: It was truly the final season that Mantle, Maris, Ford, Berra, Howard, Kubek, and Richardson would play at their peak; and it would be another 15 seasons before the Yankees would celebrate a World Series victory. The Yankees would win pennants again the next two seasons, but it was clear the dynasty was fading as the Yankees were outgunned in both of those October classics.

"We all played another few seasons," recalled Ford, "but you could see after the 1962 Series that the team was never the same. We won because McCovey hit the ball right at Bobby. After that all the line drives hit by the other teams always seemed to be past our infielders."

4

2001

The drama of the 2001 World Series between the Yankees and the Arizona Diamondbacks came as much from the horrendous events on September 11, 2001, in Lower Manhattan as from any events on the field. Terrorists attacked the Twin Towers of the World Trade Center that morning while others flew planes into the Pentagon and later open country land in Shanksville, Pennsylvania. Nearly 3,000 lives were lost, damage was in the millions, and the invulnerability of the United States was forever gone.

Baseball cancelled all its games for a week as the country dealt with the physical and emotional turmoil of the invasion of our home soil. Ninety-one regular-season games were postponed and had to be made up at the end of the regular season, forcing the post season to linger into the month of November for the first time. Play resumed gingerly on September 17 with nerves still obviously raw, a trait that persisted throughout the Division Series, the National and American League Championship Series, and the first World Series in the Arizona heat.

The 2001 Series developed into a stirring one, witnessed in person for every game by the embattled mayor of New York, Rudolph Giuliani, and dozens of other Yankee fans who believed it was their divine right to win in light of the tragedy the city had suffered. The Yankees had won the title the year before in the 2000 edition of the Subway Series against the Mets. But 2001's outcome would not go the Yankees' way. New York took a 2-1 lead into the bottom of the ninth inning of the final game with the best relief pitcher in the game's history, Mariano Rivera, on the mound with the simple aim of getting three outs. An errant throw to second base by the closer and a flair single to center anchored a two-run rally in the bottom of the ninth inning by the Diamondbacks, which won the Series for Arizona and broke the hearts of the Yankees faithful.

The series opener did not go smoothly for New York. Mike Mussina, obtained as a free agent from Baltimore for the 2001 season, got off to an embarrassing start as he was slapped around by the Diamondbacks in a 9-1 rout. Curt Schilling, who would go on to much more success and fame in Boston three years later, won the opener with ease after being given a large scoring cushion. His left-handed running mate, Randy Johnson, 21-6 with a 2.49 ERA that season for Arizona, took care of the second game with a splendid 4-0 shutout over Andy Pettitte and the Yankees. Through two games, the Yankees had collected just six hits.

Roger Clemens was handed the ball for Game 3 at Yankee Stadium. Despite being well on his way to 300 wins and certain Hall of Fame immortality, Clemens had often been less than dominant in postseason play. His most ignominious setback had come as a youngster in 1986 when he failed to hold a 3-2 lead against the Mets in the sixth game of the Fall Classic. New York battled back in the tenth inning of that game, noted by Bill

Buckner's error on a Mookie Wilson roller at first base, to win 6-5 and lock up the Series the next day.

Clemens came to the Yankees in 1999 with the sole purpose (other than increasing his bank account) of playing on a World Series winner, about the only feat left unfulfilled in his glorious career.

"That's why I'm here," he told the press as he put on a Yankee uniform for the first time. "I want that World Series ring."

He earned it as the Yankees defeated Atlanta in a four-game sweep in 1999. In 2000, after being defeated twice in the American League Division Series, Clemens rebounded to with superb work the rest of the playoffs: 17 innings pitched, three hits allowed, and 24 strikeouts. In 2001, with his team down 2-0 in the World Series, Clemens answered the call. He gave up only one run in seven innings in one of the grittiest performances ever turned in by a 39-year-old pitcher.

Clemens turned the final two innings over to Mariano Rivera, who closed it out with two scoreless innings to preserve a 2-1 victory.

"I have had a lot of good World Series performances, but my greatest Series thrill is still my first one in 1996. I wasn't even the closer then," said Rivera late in 2006. "I was just the setup man to (John) Wetteland. For me it wasn't the statistics. It was just being in the World Series. Imagine a kid from Panama with my poor background walking into Yankee Stadium for a Series game. No thrill could match that."

The suspense remained for a Game 4 matchup on Halloween eve. Tino Martinez hit a two-run, two-out ninth-inning homer off Arizona reliever Byung-Hyun Kim, the submarine-throwing Korean right-hander, to rally the Yankees to a 3-3 tie. Derek Jeter's tenth-inning solo homer, also off Kim, gave New York a walk-off win. The shot occurred shortly after midnight, giving the Yankee captain the lasting nickname Mr. November as the month turned. It was a nod to Mr. October, Reggie Jackson, and his explosive batting performance in the

1977 World Series.

Scott Brosius, another clutch Yankee performer, repeated Martinez's feat the next night with a ninth-inning, two-run homer—again off Kim—to knot the game at two and send it to extra innings. Alfonso Soriano won it in the 12th inning with a base hit to give New York a 3-2 win in Game 5.

The Yankees had their three games-to-two lead. Only one more remained for the emotional victory. A 6-foot-10 left-hander stood in their way: Randy Johnson. The Diamondbacks responded to the pressure with a smashing victory. They clubbed Andy Pettitte and the Yankees 15-2 to send the series to a seventh game. At least, the Yankees thought, they were through with Johnson as he recorded his second triumph.

Rivera, a quiet man who usually spends his pregame time reading his Bible, asked the team for its attention before they took the field at Bank One Ballpark in Phoenix for the finale.

"We're going to win tonight," he simply said.

It was the first time any of his teammates could remember the relief pitcher addressing the team in a group setting. He usually led the team by example, not words.

The Yankees took a 2-1 lead into the eighth inning in what had been a nailbiter between Clemens and Schilling, both of whom were pitching well. Clemens had already turned over the game to reliever Mike Stanton in the seventh, and Rivera entered in the eighth to record the game's final six outs.

Arizona skipper Bob Brenly went to his ace as well with two outs in the eighth—except this ace wasn't a reliever by trade. Johnson, pitching with no day's rest, induced a fly ball from Chuck Knoblauch to end the inning. The decision to go with Johnson was a bold one, but seemed pointless for Arizona as Rivera responded by retiring the Diamondbacks in the bottom of the eighth on three strikeouts. Johnson set the heart of the Yankees lineup down in order in the ninth, setting the stage for Rivera, who needed just three outs and was clinging to a one-run lead.

First baseman Mark Grace led off for Arizona with a line

single to center off Rivera. Joe Torre, the Yankee skipper, wasn't terribly concerned on the bench.

"I had so much confidence in Rivera that I never bothered to worry when Mo allowed a man or two to get on. I knew somehow he would get out of it," Torre said.

David Dellucci was sent in to run for the slow-footed Grace. Damien Miller bunted back to the mound to advance the tying run to second. Then the 2001 World Series turned in an instant: Rivera fielded the bunt, spun, and threw to Soriano, covering second. The ball sailed high and wide of Soriano as he lunged into the air for the throw. Both runners were safe on Rivera's error.

Jay Bell was next up. He bunted back to Rivera again in an attempt to advance the runners, but this time Rivera fired to Brosius at third and retired Dellucci, the lead runner, for the first out of the inning. Journeyman Tony Womack then lined Rivera's fastball to right for a double. Miller scored the tying run and Bell raced to third base as the go-ahead run. The next batter was Craig Counsell, the weak-hitting but pesky shortstop. Rivera threw a low inside pitch that caught Counsell on the foot, loading the bases for Arizona with slugger Luis Gonzalez due up.

Gonzalez, a high school teammate and pal of Yankee first baseman Tino Martinez, had clubbed 57 home runs during the 2001 campaign. He was a tough right-handed hitter who had been one of the heroes of Arizona's march to its first pennant with a .325 average in 162 games. Torre decided to pull his infield in to cut off the winning run.

"It's pretty tough to play for a double play," said Torre. "I just wanted to get Gonzalez out without a score. If that happened I would take my chances on Mo getting the next hitter out and keeping the game tied."

Mayor Giuliani squirmed in his front row seat, pulling tight on his Yankee cap. He was confident his favorite team would get out of the jam and bring home a World Series victory for the distraught New York fans.

Gonzalez took a pitch for a ball as Bell moved gingerly off third base. Now he was ready for the next pitch, guessing it would be Rivera's favorite, that biting cut-fastball, probably in on his hands where Rivera liked to throw it. He swung hard and the ball seemed to move off the bat in a lazy arch. Jeter, pulled in at short by orders from Torre, raced back from his position. He was still ten yards away from the baseball when it fell on the outfield grass like a wounded bird.

Bell had taken one quick look back and judged correctly that the ball would not be caught. He raced home hard and bounced on the plate with the World Series-winning run for the Arizona Diamondbacks.

"I wanted to be in that situation," Rivera, always a gentleman with the media, said after the game. "That's my situation. I couldn't finish it out."

It was a triumph that defied all sports tradition. The Diamondbacks had entered the National League as an expansion team in 1998, bringing big league baseball to the state of Arizona. Only four years later they won the National League pennant and defeated the Yankees, the most legendary of all sports teams, in a thrilling series.

Arizona general manager Joe Garagiola, Jr., the son of famed broadcaster and entertainer Joe Garagiola, had put together a splendid team anchored by two pitching giants, Johnson and Schilling. The two pitchers shared the World Series MVP award for their efforts in preventing the Yankees from winning four World Series titles in a row.

When it was all over after November 4, 2001, the Yankees returned home without the Series flag but with a great deal of respect as they battled down to the final batter of the ninth inning of Game 7 before conceding defeat. They had helped the City of New York move forward after the shock and tragedy of the events of 9/11. Most people finally realized after the series that despite the brutal attack, life would go on as normal. The Great American Pastime had survived, the Fall Classic had survived, and, certainly the country would survive, too.

5

1952

Every October TV producers roll the tape on a World Series highlight reel that is sure to include three famous events: Bill Mazeroski's title-clinching home run in 1960; Don Larsen celebrating after his perfect game in the 1956 Fall Classic; and a certain catch of an infield pop fly by Billy Martin off the bat of Jackie Robinson. Of all the plays and all the players Yankees manager Casey Stengel bragged about through his lifetime in the game, it was that gritty, sparkling catch turned in by Martin at Ebbets Field that brought more smiles to the Old Professor's face.

"The rest of them (other Yankee infielders) all stood out there like statues when the ball when up," said Stengel years later. "Only the little bantam second baseman had the sense to catch it."

Buzzie Bavasi, general manager of the Brooklyn Dodgers in

the 1950s, was once asked if his 1955 World Champions, Brooklyn's only World Series winner, was his best and favorite team.

"No," he replied, "it had to be the 1952 team. Every player on that team was at his peak and we had a lot of Hall of Famers and near-Hall of Famers on that squad."

Four Hall of Famers—Robinson, Pee Wee Reese, Duke Snider, and Roy Campanella—were enjoying their career peaks. Dodger teammates Gil Hodges, Carl Furillo, Andy Pafko, and Billy Cox also were performing brilliantly at the time. The formidable Brooklyn pitching staff featured Carl Erskine, Joe Black, Preacher Roe, and Billy Loes.

Still, the Yankees collected another title. It was Brooklyn's sixth Series loss in six attempts (the last four to the Yankees) and the fourth straight Series triumph by the Yankees under Stengel's leadership. The triumph came during a major transitional year for the Yankees, with the absence of the great Joe DiMaggio, who retired following the 1951 World Series, in center field. His brother Tom DiMaggio, the non-baseball playing brother who ran the family restaurant on Fisherman's Wharf in San Francisco, was asked why Joe retired at the relatively young age of 37.

"Don't you know?" asked Tom. "He wasn't Joe DiMaggio anymore."

A .263 average, an endless chain of injuries, and a lack of desire ended the Yankee Clipper's playing days. A 20-year-old center fielder from Commerce, Oklahoma, took over DiMaggio's spot in the Yankee lineup. The young pup, Mickey Mantle, hit .311 that season with 23 home runs.

With Mantle hitting third in the lineup, Phil Rizzuto ahead of him, and Berra at clean up, the Yankees took the field for Game 1 of the 1952 Series. Joe Black, a Brooklyn relief pitcher until the final eight days of the season, took the mound that day for the Dodgers with the task of shutting down New York. Black had pitched very well that season, posting a 15-4 record and a 2.15 ERA in his first year in the big leagues. With just two career starts under his belt, Black did what was asked of him, allowing two runs and pitching a complete game. The loss in the 4-2 defeat went to 20-game winner Allie Reynolds. Robinson, Snider, and Reese each homered for Brooklyn.

The Yankees had two powerful, intense, sneering right-handers who anchored their staff. One was Reynolds and the other was Vic Raschi. Few teams could beat the two back to back. The Dodgers couldn't, falling to Raschi in convincing fashion in Game 2. Raschi's smooth three-hitter paced the Yankees to a 7-1 win as his teammates batted around against Erskine. Mantle had three hits, Martin added a couple, and Gil McDougald homered in the win.

Preacher Roe came back for Brooklyn in the third game with a smart six-hitter in setting the Yankees down 5-3. Berra contributed to the Yankee loss when he allowed one of Tom Gorman's sinking curve balls get away from him in the top of the ninth for a passed ball. Reese and Robinson scored on the miscue to push the Brooklyn lead to 5-2, making Johnny Mize's ninth-inning, pinch-hit, solo homer off the 37-year-old Preacher an insignificant blast.

In another brilliant pitching matchup in the fourth game, Reynolds beat Black this time with a 2-0 shutout. Both teams collected just four hits, but the Yankees made theirs count. Mize, this time starting at first and batting clean up, hit his second home run of the series in the fourth, and New York tacked on an insurance run in the eighth.

The Dodgers went ahead 3-2 in games with a 6-5 11-inning win in Game 5. Erskine pitched all 11 innings for Brooklyn, an amazing feat for the slim right-hander. He allowed five runs in the fifth inning after the Dodgers had taken a 4-0 lead against Earl Blackwell. Snider, who homered earlier in the game, tied the game in the seventh with a single. Erskine, meanwhile, had found his curve ball and retired the last 19 batters he faced in the game. Snider was the hero again when his double off relief pitcher Johnny Sain put the Dodgers ahead for good in the 11th.

"That was probably the strangest game of my career," Erskine recalled many years later. "I couldn't seem to get my curve ball over the plate in the first few innings. The Yankees hit me hard in the fifth for the five runs but (manager) Charlie Dressen stayed with me."

Snider hit a pair of solo homers in Game 6 to give him four in the series, but the Yankees went ahead for good in the seventh on a Berra solo home run and Raschi's RBI single. Reynolds, who thought nothing of relieving on days he didn't start, fired bullets for an inning-plus to earn the save as New York won 3-2.

Just as it had been five years earlier in 1947, this Yankees-Dodgers Fall Classic would be decided by a seventh game. Ralph Branca and the other Dodgers who had been through the bitter losses of 1947 and 1949 looked to get even with the Yankees.

Crafty left-hander Ed Lopat, whose fastball couldn't break a pane of glass, started for the Yankees, while Black got his third start in seven days. Pitchers were made of sterner stuff then. Reynolds was called on in relief to slow down a Brooklyn rally in the fourth that tied the game 1-1. Mantle homered in the sixth, then singled in the seventh to push the Yankees' lead to 4-2 as the fans at Ebbets Field grew restless.

It was up to Raschi and his weary arm to keep the Dodgers at bay in the bottom half of the seventh. Raschi failed, loading the bases on a pair of walks and a single. "They're FOB," said broadcaster Red Barber, in his familiar style. "Full of Brooks." Stengel went to the mound and waved for left-handed reliever Bob Kuzava to relieve Raschi. Kuzava, making his first appearance of the series, would have to face Snider with just one out.

"I figured I would just be facing the left-handed hitter, Snider, and then Casey would go to the righty, Johnny Sain, for the next Brooklyn hitter, Jackie Robinson," Kuzava recalled years later. "I was throwing hard, but I always had a little control trouble. All lefthanders do. Our ball just takes off."

The count went to 3-2 on Snider. Kuzava, a lefty who could

get the ball up to the plate in the high 90s, threw a high fastball that Snider chased out of the strike zone, sending a weak popup to Joe Collins at first. Two out. Bases still loaded. The Yankees clinging to a two-run lead. The Series hanging on the line. Robinson, one of the game's greatest clutch hitters, up to bat with 33,000 fans screaming for Yankees blood.

"Casey came to the mound. I was sure he would go with Sain against Jackie. Then Yogi told Casey, 'He's throwin' good.' Casey said, 'All right, get 'em out.' Then he turned and walked away," Kuzava recalled.

The count ran to 3-2 against Robinson. The next pitch would settle the 1952 World Series. Robinson, as was his custom at the plate, ran his sweaty right hand down the side of his pants to dry out his palm. Kuzava went to his best pitch and fired a fastball just off the plate and about shoulder high to Robinson. The base runners took off with the pitch. Umpire Larry Goetz may have called it a ball to force in a run and bring Campanella to the plate. But he didn't get the chance: Robinson lunged at the pitch with an awkward swing. The ball sailed high behind the mound. Berra never took off his mask at home plate to look for it. Gil McDougald at third and Rizzuto at shortstop stayed firm near their assigned positions as the baseball began its downward trajectory. Collins kept still near the first-base bag in case anybody happened to show up there.

Only Billy Martin seemed to pay any attention to the popup. He was playing Robinson straightaway and raced to the left of the mound as the baseball sunk lower and lower.

"If I didn't get out of the way Billy would have run me over," recalled Kuzava.

Instead, the pitcher moved toward third as Billy charged for the baseball. The ball was now about a foot off the ground and ever so close to dropping safely as the Dodgers raced around the bases. Martin leaned forward—his hat now gone from his head, his eyes bulging, his hair flowing in the Brooklyn breeze, his glove just above the sacred Ebbets Field dirt—and caught the pop up.

Kuzava remembered the sound of the baseball smacking into Martin's glove for the final out of the inning. Billy carried it a few more steps as he continued racing for the dugout. Then he deposited the baseball in front of the mound as his excited teammates followed him into the dugout.

Most of the Yankees pounded Martin on the back in congratulations as he made it to the bench. He couldn't understand all the fuss. "Could you believe this?" Martin muttered to his centerfield pal, Mickey Mantle. "They pat you on the back for catching a popup."

Stengel would never forget the catch; despite a breakdown in communications between the manager and Martin after he was unceremoniously traded away from the Yankees in 1957, Stengel always bragged about the play.

"He made the catch on Robinson and you could look it up," Casey would often say when he spotted Martin across the field in some uniform other than the Yankee pinstripes. "Nobody else wanted to get it."

Despite historical lore, the play didn't end the World Series. Erskine, working in relief, kept the Yankees scoreless in the eighth and ninth innings. Kuzava matched him, however, and the Yankees earned another hard-fought championship. Bavasi's boys were left searching for their first.

"All these years later I still look back on that 1952 club and wonder why we weren't able to beat the Yankees. That was our finest team, but we hit in some bad luck that October," Bavasi said.

Stengel never could be pinned down to pick his best Yankee team among the five straight titles he won in New York from 1949-1953, or for any of the other two championships in 1956 and 1958. Yet he could always be counted on to describe his favorite play, Billy Martin's incredible, lunging catch of Robinson's popup. Kuzava admits that he still gets a kick out of watching the play as it shows up on television during modern World Series action.

"I often wonder what kind of an inning it would have

turned out to be or if I would have stayed in the game if Billy didn't catch it or if he had kicked it," said Kuzava. "We'll never know, will we?"

There have been so many dramatic plays in Yankees World Series history, so many miraculous defensive gems, so many extraordinary efforts by the players in Yankee pinstripes. As far as I'm concerned, none match Billy Martin's catch.

As Casey Stengel would often say, even to this day, thanks to the miracle of film footage, "You could look it up."

6

1996

Following the 1995 season, Buck Showalter was fired as the Yankee skipper after a dispute with owner George Steinbrenner over money and power. To fill the vacancy, the Boss searched for wide and far for the right person to take over his improving club, which had made it back to postseason play in 1995 after an absence of 13 seasons. There was no shortage of names in Steinbrenner's hopper, yet none of the candidates excited Steinbrenner.

"Why not Joe Torre?" asked Arthur Richman, a senior advisor on the Yankees and a former traveling secretary and public relations director of the hometown New York Mets when Torre was that team's manager.

"Who is he?" Steinbrenner innocently asked.

Steinbrenner suggested that Richman call Torre at his St. Louis home, bring him to New York for an interview, and set up a conference call with other Yankee executives.

Torre had been born and raised in Brooklyn, but he rooted on the New York Giants as a kid. His older brother Frank Torre, later a first baseman for the old Milwaukee Braves, often accompanied Joe to Giants games against the Brooklyn Dodgers at Ebbets Field. Joe Torre's only Yankee Stadium memory was as a fan at Larsen's 1956 World Series perfect game.

Torre was named manager of the lowly Mets in 1977, then managed the Atlanta Braves, served as a broadcaster with the California Angels, and managed the Cardinals starting in 1990. (He was fired in June of 1995 while Showalter was riding high with the Yankees.) Torre was unemployed when Richman called in late October to invite him to a session with the Boss. He was announced as Yankee manager on November 2, 1995. "CLUE-LESS JOE," read the headline in the *New York Daily News* about the signing of Torre as Yankee skipper after such legendary Yankee managers as Joe McCarthy, Casey Stengel, and Ralph Houk.

Torre won 92 games with the Yankees that first season as the team finished atop its division for the first time since the 1981 Yankees had won the pennant and made it to the World Series. One year after being defeated in the Division Series by the Mariners, the Yankees defeated the Rangers three games to one in the ALDS, then advanced to the World Series after a four games-to-one defeat of the Orioles. Their opponent in the Fall Classic was the Braves, who had won 96 games that season and rallied back from a three games-to-one deficit in the National League Championship Series to defeat the Cardinals.

The Braves remained hot to start the World Series, winning the first two games behind a 12-1 opening-day romp for John Smoltz and a 4-0 second-game shutout by Greg Maddux and flame throwing reliever Mark Wohlers. Braves pitchers baffled the Yankees, allowing just 11 hits—and only two for extra bases—over Games 1 and 2.

Atlanta center fielder, Andruw Jones, triggered the opening-game win with two tremendous homers at Yankee Stadium. At just 19 years old, he became the youngest player to ever hit a World Series homer, edging out 20-year-old Mickey Mantle for that honor after Mickey hit the first of his 18 World Series homers in 1952.

"I never thought it could happen this fast," said Jones, who had only 106 big league at-bats coming into the World Series.

With the series returning to Atlanta for Games 3 through 5, Jones and the Braves hoped to keep their postseason win streak alive. Before the Yankees departed for Fulton County Stadium, Steinbrenner visited his manager in the clubhouse, anxious to show his concern.

"Don't worry, Boss," Torre said. "We'll get them down there."

Steinbrenner, as volatile a baseball boss as ever existed, couldn't get any words out of his mouth. He just stared at his rookie skipper in amazement.

David Cone gave Steinbrenner reason to relax by turning in his finest Yankee Series performance in the third game of the October Classic. He allowed the Braves only one run in six innings before turning the game over to rookie set-up man Mariano Rivera and veteran closer John Wetteland for the 5-2 victory. Bernie Williams, a rare Yankees organization player, padded New York's 2-1 lead with a two-run home run in the eighth inning.

The fourth game of the series was marked by one of those plays that, because they occur in the World Series under the brightest lights of baseball, can change not just a game or the series but a player's life. Jim Leyritz was a Yankees backup catcher who swung for the fences almost every time at bat. Once in a while he connected.

The Yankees were down 6-0 to the Braves in the sixth inning, teetering on the verge of falling behind three games to one on the road. New York had picked up three runs in the top of the sixth on three singles, a walk, and an error. The team went down quietly in the seventh, but then forced the issue in the eighth. Chuck Hayes led off with an infield single to third against Mark Wohlers, the Braves' hard-throwing right-handed closer. Darryl Strawberry followed with a single, then Mariano Duncan hit a ground ball to short to force Strawberry out at second. With runners at the corners and one out, Leyritz stepped to the plate.

"We wanted a long ball," recalled Torre, "and Jimmy was certainly capable of it."

"That's all I was thinking of as I came to the plate," Leyritz said. "I know you are not supposed to think about hitting homers because then you swing at bad pitches. I just told myself to swing hard."

Wohlers fired his best fastball on a 2-2 count and Leyritz swung his hardest. The ball sailed on a line over the left-field wall as the Yankees bounced out of the dugout to celebrate the game-tying homer. Leyritz was pounded hard by his mates as he jogged into the dugout.

"I loved the game. I played hard, but I knew I wasn't going to be a great player or an immortal Yankee. I think nobody can forget me now after I hit that one," said Leyritz, now a Florida broadcaster.

The Yankees rallied for two runs in the tenth on a bases-loaded walk by Wade Boggs and a run-scoring groundball by Hayes that wasn't fielded cleanly. Wetteland shut down the Braves in the bottom half of the inning and the series was suddenly tied at two games each, setting up a matchup between Andy Pettitte and Smoltz.

Pettitte, who had won 21 games that season as a 24-year-old in just his second year, pitched brilliantly for 8 ⅓ innings, allowing five hits and no runs. The performance made up for the drubbing he had suffered in Game 1 of the Series. Smoltz nearly matched him for eight innings, allowing just four hits while striking out 10. But Smoltz allowed an unearned run in the fourth, the difference in a tight ballgame. Wetteland entered in the ninth after Chipper Jones led off the inning with a double, then moved to third on a ground out. The right-hander induced Javy Lopez into a weak ground out that failed to advance Jones at third, then two batters later retired Luis Polonia on a fly ball to the right-center gap to end the game.

After being down two games to none and going on the road for three, the Yankees were returning to the Stadium for Game 6 with a one-game lead. It was reason to be optimistic, yet Torre could hardly concentrate on the matter at hand. His older brother, Frank, was in Columbia Presbyterian Hospital in Manhattan for heart transplant surgery. Torre raced to the hospital as soon as the team got home. His brother, who had been suffering heart problems for many years and at the age of 64 was told that only a new heart could save his life, was in critical condition following the surgery.

"He was wearing his Yankee cap," Torre said of his brother, "and he was already offering me advice on the pitching matchups. I knew he would be OK."

As Frank Torre recovered from his life-threatening trauma, Joe Torre returned to matters at hand. Lefthander Jimmy Key took the mound against Maddux for Game 6. Braves manager Bobby Cox, once a Yankee third baseman himself, thought his team was still in good position despite being down a game. He had Maddux for Game 6 and Tom Glavine ready for the finale.

It was not to be.

The Yankees pounced on Maddux in the third inning on RBI base hits by Jeter, Williams, and backup catcher Joe Girardi, a notoriously light hitter. Key, meanwhile, allowed the Braves only one run into the sixth inning; from there, the durable pen took over with a 3-0 lead.

"Key gave us just about what we expected," Torre said later. "We knew the bullpen was a strong part of our team. If we could have a lead into the sixth or seventh inning we figured we could shut them down."

Rivera, who would become the Yankees closer the following season as Wetteland moved on, was splendid for two innings. With a 3-1 lead, Torre turned the game over to Wetteland in the ninth.

"One of the secrets of the Series," Torre said, " is you have to play the games the way you played them during the season. You only ask the guys to do in October what they have been doing all season. Wetteland was our closer so with a lead we gave him the ball."

Torre was hardly speaking from experience at that point: He had never been in a World Series as a player, and could not steer the Mets, the Braves, or the Cardinals into a Series as a skipper. Wetteland nearly made his manager look a fool. The hard thrower suffered from bouts of control trouble at the worst of times, including this instance. After striking out Andruw Jones to open the frame, he surrendered a pair of singles then notched his second strikeout of the inning. Marquis Grissom stepped into the batters' box with two outs and runners on first and third. Wetteland lost the battle as Grissom poked a single through the hole between first and second to bring the Braves to within one run of New York.

Now it was the big right-hander facing the small infielder Mark Lemke for the final out of the Series. Lemke was a pesky hitter with great control of the bat and an uncanny ability to hit the hardest throwers in the games. Wetteland got ahead quickly with a couple of strikes, threw a slider outside, and then missed on a high fastball. Wetteland took a deep breath, stared down at Girardi's fastball sign, fired as hard as he could to the plate, and watched Lemke swing hard at the outside pitch. It floated on a looping curve toward the stands behind third base. Its arc shifted suddenly, curving back as Wetteland pointed over to third baseman Charlie Hayes. The journeyman infielder tracked the baseball as it softly sailed down into his glove in foul territory as his feet left the ground. He bounced once or twice upon landing, keeping the ball secured, and then rose to his feet and took off for home plate.

An explosive demonstration filled the Stadium turf with celebrating players, executives, and a few fans who made it over the rails. The event will be forever marked by a ride around the Stadium by Wade Boggs, a long-suffering Boston third baseman before his move to the Bronx. Boggs mounted a New York City policeman's horse and tramped around the Stadium grass. If any fan ever questions whether money is the single motivation for big league success, they need only stare at Boggs as he circled the historic field with the New York City mounted police. No grin could be wider.

The Yankees were the champions of the baseball world for the 23rd time in the team's history, a feat unequalled in any sport by any team. In a few days they would all gather again in open cars and large trucks for that famous ride down Broadway in Manhattan. It was the same path followed by Charles Lindbergh in the 1920s, Generals Douglas MacArthur and Dwight Eisenhower after times of war, John Glenn and his astronaut pals after the space orbits, and the New York Mets in 1969.

While the teenagers gathered in the Lower Broadway streets and screamed "Jeter, Jeter, Jeter," at the handsome kid shortstop of the Yankees, other fans threw confetti from high office windows, sent balloons flying over the cars, and pushed autograph requests into the vehicles. Not surprisingly, it was the kid from Brooklyn— now grown to full New York sports iconic status— Manager Joe Torre who seemed to get the most attention from the adoring crowd. They recognized that under Torre's leadership and with a little help from Steinbrenner's money, the Yankees had won the World Series again after an 18-year break.

Torre made a warm speech at the City Hall welcoming ceremonies with Mayor Rudolph Giuliani at his side.

"This is a great day for the Yankees and a great day for the City of New York," he said as thousands cheered.

Each World Series has its own status, its own set of memories, its own joys for the devoted fans. If the 1996 World Series triumph by the Yankees wasn't the most thrilling collection of games it may well have been the most joyous for devotees of the team. Eighteen years seemed far too long for any fan of the Yankees to wait before they could honestly hold up a pointing index finger and shout aloud, "We're number one."

Finally, they were.

7

1958

The 1958 World Series was the last of Casey Stengel's seven triumphs for the Yankees in the Fall Classic. It marked only the second time in Series history that a team came back from a 3-1 deficit to win a seven-game series (Pittsburgh had done it against Washington in 1925). It also gave the Yankees ultimate revenge for the devastating loss against the same Milwaukee Braves the previous October.

Bullet Bob Turley picked up two wins and a save in the series—all in a span of just four days. "It was a different game then," Turley recalled from his Florida home. "Just because I was a starter didn't mean I couldn't get into the game as a relief pitcher. Casey had a lot of confidence in me. . . ."

Turley won the Cy Young Award as the game's best pitcher that year with a 21-7 regular-season mark and 19 complete games in 31 starts. He also helped the Yankees win a lot of other games thanks to his masterful skill of reading the opposing pitcher and relaying signs to his teammates at the plate.

Stengel, who had first played in a Series as a member of the 1916 Brooklyn Dodgers against Babe Ruth's Boston Red Sox, was edgy coming into the World Series in 1958. The Brooklyn Dodgers had defeated the Yankees in 1955 and the Yankees came back to beat them in 1956. The Braves had won the seventh game of the 1957 Series to take the title. The 68-year-old Stengel knew only a Series victory could soften that blow.

Milwaukee won the opener 4-3 in ten innings in the kind of game expected after a long, 154-game season. Warren Spahn, the future Hall of Famer who would claim baseball's title as the game's winningest left-hander, went all the way for the victory; starter Whitey Ford and reliever Ryne Duren pitched for the Yankees. Singles by Joe Adcock, Del Crandall, and Billy Bruton off Duren won the game for Milwaukee in the final inning.

Duren took the loss hard: "I did what I always did after every bad game," he said. "I drank away my sorrow."

Duren, a recovering alcoholic now working with others with similar problems, also had another major deficit as a hard-throwing right-handed reliever—poor eyesight.

"I couldn't see a thing," he remembered. "There were times when I got into a game and I was woozy from the drink and unable to see with my bad eyes."

He had a regular habit of entering the game and throwing the first warm-up pitch behind his catcher and off the screen in Yankee Stadium. Fans blamed the errant throw on his bad eyes hidden behind coke bottle glasses. The fans always roared.

"They just expected that from me," he said.

The Braves pushed to a 2-0 series lead with a 13-3 victory in Milwaukee's County Stadium. They exploded for seven runs in the first inning off Turley and reliever Duke Maas. Billy Bruton homered to lead off the bottom of the first and ignite the Braves offense. Milwaukee starting pitcher Lew Burdette even got into the action in the first, hitting a three-run homer off Maas. In the latter innings the Braves piled on five more runs to stretch their lead to 13-2. Mickey Mantle hit his second home run of the game in the bottom of the ninth in a lost cause. Hank Bauer, who would become New York's hitting star in the series, also homered that inning as Burdette tired in the game's final frame.

"Burdette was a tough pitcher with all that tricky stuff he threw," Bauer said, licking his fingers to indicate Burdette may have been throwing spitters. Speaking at the Yankees Old Timer's game in 2006, Bauer continued: "He had good control for a lefty and I was glad I could get one off him."

The Yankees had dug themselves into another hole, but were heading home for Games 3 through 5. Don Larsen was the Yankee starter for Game 3 against veteran Bob Rush. Bauer broke the scoreless tie in the fifth with a pop-fly single to right that scored two Yankee runs. He locked up the 4-0 victory in the seventh with a two-run homer after Enos Slaughter drew a pinch-hit walk.

"That was a big hit," Bauer said of his homer, "because it gave us the win and made sure we didn't fall three games back."

The Braves seemed to lay claim on their second championship in a row against the Yankees with a 3-0, two-hit shutout by Spahn in the fourth game. Spahn, who later pitched for the Mets at the age of 43 (his catcher for one game was Yogi Berra at age 40 as part of the game's oldest battery), always considered that victory his finest game.

"I pitched a couple of no-hitters but this was the World Series," he once said. "It was also against the Yankees, the most famous team in baseball and against Casey Stengel. You know I pitched for Casey before and after he was a genius."

Spahn was on Stengel's horrible 1942 Boston Braves and also pitched again for Stengel on the terrible 1965 Mets. Ford was Spahn's Game 4 opponent in a battle of two future lefty Hall of Famers. He pitched effectively, but was outdone by the sun in left field. Norm Siebern, playing his first full season for the Yankees, lost a couple fly balls in the sun, and the Braves scored a couple easy runs on the way to building a three games-to-one advantage. Berra, who would later play some left field himself, once said of the shadows, "It gets late early out there." Siebern could understand that well.

Facing elimination, New York rallied around Turley, who shut out the Braves 7-0 on five hits. Gil McDougald homered in the third for Turley's only needed run. Elston Howard, the first black Yankee, patrolled left after Siebern's miscues the previous game. Howard made a diving catch of Red Schoendienst's looping fly ball in the sixth inning to choke off a Milwaukee rally. Defensive gems don't get much attention in regular-season play, but the World Series catches of Willie Mays in 1954, Howard in 1958, and Tommie Agee and Ron Swoboda in 1969 have lived on in fame. Energized by Howard's defense, the Yankees exploded for six runs in their half of the sixth inning to knock Burdette out of the game and give Turley his first series win.

The sixth game was a beauty. Spahn and Ford both started on short rest. Warren outlasted Whitey, who was removed in the second inning after struggling in both the first and second frames. Spahn, meanwhile, lasted into the tenth inning. With the score tied at 2-2 in the top of the tenth, a lead-off homer by McDougald and singles by Howard and Berra chased Spahn from the game. Reliever Don McMahon then surrendered an RBI hit to Skowron to put the Yankees up 4-2.

Duren took the mound in the bottom of the inning, entering his fifth inning of relief work that game. Shortstop Johnny Logan walked with one out, moved up on Hank Aaron's single, and scored on Joe Adcock's single to bring the Braves to within one run. Adcock's hit moved the tying run, in the form of Aaron, to third base. That was enough for Stengel. He replaced Duren with none other than Game 5 starter Turley. Bullet Bob overpowered Frank Torre with a 100-mile-per-hour heater. Torre could only hit a soft liner to second baseman McDougald for the final out of the game.

Turley now had won the fifth game and saved the sixth. Would he also start the seventh and deciding game? No. Stengel went with the Perfect Man, Larsen, as his seventh-game starter.

Turley was instructed to stay warm in the bullpen, just in case.

A pair of errors by Braves first baseman Torre in the second inning gave the Yankees an early 2-1 edge in the seventh game. Turley was called upon again in the third inning as Larsen found himself in trouble for the second time in the game. Turley pitched the Yankees out of hot water and remained in the game to pitch in the fourth inning and beyond.

In the sixth, Turley surrendered a game-tying home run to Crandall. The score remained tied at 2-2 heading into the eighth, with Burdette still on the mound for Milwaukee. He retired McDougald to start the inning, then struck out Mantle looking. Berra kept the inning alive with a double to right, then Howard smacked Burdette's 2-2 pitch on a line into left-center field for a tie-breaking single. Andy Carey then slapped a single to right field moving Howard, a notoriously slow runner, to second. That brought Skowron, New York's poor-fielding, great-hitting first baseman, to the plate.

Burdette, a Yankee farmhand as a young pitcher, had gotten his revenge on his old team with three winning pitching performances in 1957 World Series. Now in 1958 he could embarrass the Yankees again with a seventh-game victory. Skowron had other ideas. He saw a high outside waste pitch on a 0-1 count and slugged it over the wall in right field as he had done so many times during the previous four seasons.

The three-run blast gave the Yankees a 6-2 lead with Turley still on the mound. He retired the last six outs to preserve the four-run lead and wrap up the victory. It was Stengel's seventh World Series title in nine tries. New York had plenty of outstanding hitters in the series: Bauer, with a .323 mark, four home runs, and eight RBIs; Skowron with seven RBIs; and McDougald with a .321 average and two home runs. But this was certainly the Series of Bullet Bob Turley. He pitched 16 ⅓ innings in four games, won Games 5 and 7, saved Game 6, and shut the Braves down with a single run in almost seven innings of relief in the deciding game.

The Yankees had their revenge victory over the Braves and

Stengel, who had once managed in Milwaukee had evened the score over the 1957 winners.

"I like 'em all," Stengel once told me about his World Series victories, "but the 1958 win over the Braves was most splendid. After all they had beaten us the year before and when we went down everybody thought they would beat us again. My guys thought otherwise."

Stengel could hardly know this would be his final World Series triumph. Looking back it was clear that it was his favorite.

8

1950

How could a four-game series sweep be considered one of the greatest October Classics in Yankees' history? Only if was the 1950 World Series between the Yankees and the Philadelphia Phillies' Whiz Kids, who earned their nickname due to a talented core of young players.

"It was the only one I was ever in," said Robin Roberts, the anchor of the Whiz Kids pitching staff at the age of 23 and a future Hall of Fame pitcher, "and I thought it was a great and dramatic series.

"It was my first 20-game season (he won 20 games six times in a row along the way to 286 career wins) and we didn't win the pennant until the last day. We were pretty high and excited when we took the field in Philadelphia for the first game."

Philadelphia manager Eddie Sawyer, an old mathematics

teacher, had figured Roberts was his strong boy and used him that way. Roberts pitched in three of the team's final six games of the regular season while left-hander Curt Simmons, a 17-game winner, was lost to military service with the start of the Korean war. Roberts had beaten the Dodgers the previous Sunday on a three-run homer by Dick Sisler in the top of the tenth. The Yankees, who had won the 1949 pennant on the last day of the season by beating Boston (Hello, Curse of the Bambino), had an easier time in 1950, edging Detroit by three games. They got an immediate break in the World Series opener when Sawyer shockingly named Jim Konstanty as his starter against New York's Vic Raschi. Roberts had pitched ten tough innings three days prior, and his manager felt he would be stronger with a normal amount of rest between starts.

Konstanty, one of the oldest Phillies at age 33, hadn't started a game in four years and had never started one for the Phillies. He was primarily the team's ace reliever, having record 16 wins, 22 saves, and a 2.66 ERA that season.

"We had a lot of confidence in him," remembered Roberts. "He had been a big guy for us all year, threw very hard, and had a lot of guts. We weren't concerned that he wasn't a starter. He was a pitcher."

Konstanty avoided trouble through the first three innings, but the Yankees scored off him in the fourth after Bobby Brown doubled to lead off the inning. The Phillies could only collect two hits off Raschi, singles by third baseman Willie "Puddin' Head" Jones and catcher Andy Seminick—both coming in the fifth inning. Raschi allowed just one other base runner on a walk in setting the Phillies down 1-0 in the opener.

"We were all pretty tired by then after the tough pennant race, so it wasn't too surprising that we didn't hit in the opener," said Roberts. "I thought I would be strong enough now for a good game (in Game 2). If we got a few runs we could tie the Series up. It didn't quite work out that way."

Roberts and Allie Reynolds battled in another thrilling game through nine innings. The Yankees scored a run off

Roberts in the second, and Philadelphia tied it 1-1 in the fifth with their first tally of the series. The Yankees had Roberts on the ropes several times in the game as they collected ten hits; but the team often failed to come through with a big hit. As the game headed to extra innings, the New York offense redeemed itself. Roberts faced the aging Yankee Clipper, Joe DiMaggio, to lead off the tenth. DiMaggio, 35 years old by now and enjoying a comeback season after his injury-ravaged 1949 campaign, drove Roberts' 1-1 fastball on a line over the wall in short left-center field.

"I had handled him up until that last at-bat," said Roberts. "Maybe with all the pitching I had done in the last few weeks of the season and this tough 10-inning game I didn't have the same zip on my fastball."

The home run put the Yankees up 2-1 in the tenth inning and Reynolds, who never seemed to tire on this day, set the Phillies down in the bottom half of the inning for the victory. Less than two hours after the game ended, both teams were on the train for New York City for Game 3 the very next day at Yankee Stadium. Rizzuto, Berra, and McDougald car-pooled from Yankee Stadium to their New Jersey homes while DiMaggio hustled downtown for a late dinner at Toots Shor's fabled restaurant on West 51st street in Manhattan.

"The Clipper was in a pretty good mood when he came in," Shor once recalled. "I was from Philadelphia and I went down to see [Game 2]. It was great fun. He had his private table in the back of the joint and a lot of the newspaper crumb bums came around to interview him."

DiMaggio wouldn't say much because the series was only half over. The Yankees would have to take on a veteran left-hander, Ken Heintzelman, the next day. The Phillies, with only one run to their name in the series, were anxious to get after Yankee junkballer Eddie Lopat. (The term may be a bit harsh, but Lopat couldn't throw a ball through a wall the way Reynolds and Raschi could.)

"A lot of us hadn't ever seen Yankee Stadium before, and

that was pretty exciting in itself," Roberts said. "We hadn't scored any runs but we felt that our offense would come alive against Lopat and we could take advantage of our running speed in the big, open park."

Stengel, always thinking of the angles, decided to go with Lopat in the Stadium because he gave up a lot of fly balls that his outfield teammates could catch much easier in the Bronx than they might in the tight confines of Philadelphia's Shibe Park.

"I already knew I was pitching the next day," remembered Whitey Ford. "If Lopat got through the third game I would have a chance to close the Series out with a sweep in the fourth game. That was pretty exciting stuff for a kid from Queens."

The third game of the series was another thrilling contest in doubt into the bottom of the ninth inning. The Phillies doubled their series scoring output in with a run in the sixth and another in the seventh to take a 2-1 lead into the eighth behind Heintzelman, who had allowed just four hits in the game. The left-hander suddenly lost control with his team just six outs from a win; with two outs in the inning, he walked Jerry Coleman, Berra, and DiMaggio to load the bases. Game 1 starter and season-long reliever Jim Konstanty came in to get the inning's final out. He appeared to do just that as Brown hit a routine ground ball to shortstop Granny Hamner, but Hamner choked the ball, dropped it, and couldn't make a play on the speedy Brown. The error scored the tying run, but Konstanty stopped the bleeding by inducing Mize into a foul flyout.

With the game tied in the top of the ninth, Hamner redeemed himself with a leadoff double to the gap in left-center field. He was sacrificed to third, and following an intentional walk Konstanty was due up. Sawyer went for the win, sending up Dick Whitman, a former Dodger who had played in the World Series the year before against the Yankees, to hit for Konstanty. Whitman hit a grounder to Joe Collins, who was subbed in for defense at first, and Collins fired home to nab Hamner. The return throw to first was too late for the double play, leaving runners on first and second with two outs. Reliever Tom Ferrick recorded the final out, sending the game to the bottom of the ninth still tied at 2-2.

Veteran Jimmy Bloodworth, who replaced second baseman Mike Goliat, got the Phillies into quick trouble in the ninth. He couldn't handle a tricky ground ball off the bat of Gene Woodling, which went for a two-out hit. Then Bloodworth knocked down a Rizzuto liner but couldn't make a play on the ball, giving New York a runner in scoring position at second. That brought up Coleman, the World War II Marine flying ace who would be called back into service when the Korean War heated up in 1952. Phillies right-hander Russ Meyer, who would later be part of Brooklyn's only world championship team in 1955, was on the mound.

"I just wanted to make contact," Coleman, now a broadcaster with the San Diego Padres, remembered. "In a spot like that you just want to make sure you don't strike out."

Coleman hit Meyer's 2-2 pitch into left center field for a base hit. Woodling, the chunky Yankees outfielder long platooned with Bauer in left field, chugged all the way around from second base to score the game-winning run for a 3-2 victory, much to the delight of the 64,500 fans in attendance.

The Yankees now had an insurmountable 3-0 lead. No World Series team had ever blown such a lead in the 47-year history of the Fall Classic. The team's 21-year-old wunderkind, Whitey Ford, had won nine straight games after joining the Yankees from Kansas City on June 29. He got his Yankee chance after writing Stengel a letter explaining how he could help the skipper's pitching staff. Stengel was so impressed with the cocky lefty that he brought him to New York despite general manager George Weiss' contention that he wasn't ready. Weiss was more concerned that he would have to raise Ford's $3,500 minor league salary to the big league standard of $5,000. Ford proved to be worth the extra money.

The Yankees got two early runs off rookie pitcher Bob Miller in the first inning and three more, including a Berra home run, off ubiquitous Jim Konstanty in the sixth. None other than Robin Roberts finished out the game for the Phillies, who could do little against Ford. The rookie coasted along into the ninth on a smooth five-hitter with a double by Puddin' Head Jones the lone Philadelphia extra-base hit. Jones started the ninth against Ford with a single and Del Ennis, the Phillies' RBI guy, was hit by a pitch. Stengel began to squirm on the bench. He wanted the series over quickly so he could adjourn to his usual table at Toots Shor's for some steaks, booze, and conversation with his newspaper pals. After Ford retired Ennis on a ground-ball forceout at second, he struck out Hamner for the second out.

"I still felt strong," said Ford. "I wanted to get that last out. Casey came to the mound with Andy Seminick at the plate. I convinced him I was still pitching well and had good stuff. Yogi mumbled the same thing. Casey trusted Yogi more than me, a mere rookie, and let me stay in against Seminick."

With runners at the corners, Whitey unleashed a curve ball on the inside part of the plate. Seminick hit a routine fly ball to left field where Woodling, battling the late afternoon sun, gave chase.

"I could see he was having trouble with it from the start," Ford recalled.

Woodling dropped the ball, allowing two runners to score. Seminick was safe at first base. Casey stayed on the bench, certain that his young left hander could handle the weak-hitting Goliat for the final out.

"I wasn't nervous," Ford recalled. "I just wanted to end it with Goliat. Yogi squatted down behind the plate and gave me the sign. I figured this would be the last pitch of the game."

It wasn't the last pitch of the game, but it was the last pitch of Ford's 1950 World Series experience. Goliat pulled a ground ball just past Rizzuto for a hit. Before the ball reached Woodling in left field, Stengel was on his way to the mound.

"I couldn't talk him out of it this time," Ford said. "He just said, 'Give me the ball.' I turned it over to him and started walking off the mound. Some of the fans were booing him as he walked off, but he closed the space behind me and we both sort of walked off together as Reynolds came in."

Reynolds, the guy the Yankees called "SuperChief" for his Native American background, took over the mound despite tossing 10 innings in Game 2 just two days prior. The batter was backup catcher Stan Lopata. He ran the count to 1-2 against Reynolds, then whiffed on a heater high and inside to finish the game.

The Yankees had swept the Phillies four games to none, the first Series sweep since the 1939 Yankees had swept the Cincinnati Reds for their record-breaking fourth championship in a row. Their record would be broken by another Yankees run of five straight under Stengel from 1949-1953.

"I was disappointed I didn't get a chance to finish the game," Ford remembered, "but the idea is to win. I guess I felt pretty confident of that when Casey brought in Reynolds."

It was a four-game sweep for the Yankees and Philadelphia had scored all of five runs in those tight games. Sweeps usually aren't thrilling Series events, yet this one certainly was. A couple of Philadelphia hits here and there and a couple of Yankee mistakes and it could have been a four-game sweep the other way. For that reason, the 1950 World Series remains high on my list of thrilling Fall Classics.

9

1951

Berra, McDougald, and Rizzuto got up from their upper-deck seats at the Polo Grounds after the eighth inning of the final playoff game between the Brooklyn Dodgers and the New York Giants on October 3, 1951. Brooklyn led 4-1.

"It looked like the Dodgers had it won," Berra recalled. "I wanted to beat the traffic home."

As Berra drove to his fashionable Tudor home in the fancy section of Montclair, New Jersey, Bobby Thomson hit the home run forever after known as The Shot Heard 'Round the World. The Giants won the pennant and would open the 1951 World Series against the Yankees the next afternoon at Yankee Stadium. It would be the last of the Subway Series between the teams just a short walk apart across the Harlem River, the Yankees of Bronx, New York, and the Giants of the Polo Grounds, Manhattan.

The 1951 Yankees had won their third straight pennant under the leadership of Stengel, once considered a clown from his comical Brooklyn days but now revered as the Old Professor who guided the Yankees back to their former greatness. Leo Durocher, with a little help from a sign-stealing system in the Polo Grounds consisting of a telescope and an electric buzzer, had led the Giants to a 37-7 mark in the final weeks of the 1951 season. Now the two New York teams would meet in the Series for the sixth time. Stengel had been a member of the Giants the first three times the teams battled for a championship in 1921-23.

The series turned to the Yankees' favor thanks to an unscheduled day of rest, caused by a huge rainstorm after the Giants had taken a 2-1 lead in games. Mother Nature was as important for the Yankees as the hitting of Brown (.357) and Rizzuto (.320), and the final homer of DiMaggio's career. The Giants had won one of the most dramatic pennant races in the game's history, but it left their pitching staff, mainly anchor starters Sal Maglie (23-6) and Larry Jansen (23-11), spent at World Series time. Both had pitched in the final playoff game against Brooklyn a day earlier.

Durocher went to left-hander Dave Koslo as his opening-game starter against Reynolds for the Yankees. Reynolds had pitched two no-hitters in 1951, a 1-0 game against Cleveland in July and an 8-0 triumph over the Red Sox in September. Ted Williams had fouled out "twice" to end the second no-hit gem. He hit a foul near the Yankee dugout with two out in the ninth inning. Yogi Berra dropped it. Williams then hit another spinning foul, much more difficult to catch, on the next pitch. Berra made that catch after a long run and short lunge.

Reynolds was anything but unhittable in the series opener. He surrendered eight hits, walked seven, and gave up five runs in six innings. Koslo handled the Yankee batting order and World War II veteran Monte Irvin and LSU superstar athlete Alvin Dark took care of the offense as the Giants cruised to a 5-1 victory.

"I remember that game like it was yesterday," said Irvin during Hall of Fame induction weekend in July of 2006. "I had popped up the day before in the ninth inning just before Bobby (Thomson) homered, so I wanted to make up for it. Reynolds threw hard but I was a fastball hitter, so that was perfect for me."

Irvin collected a triple, three singles, and the first World Series steal of home since 1928, and Dark smashed his decisive three-run homer in the sixth off Reynolds.

"The steal was the play I really enjoyed. It wasn't even close and it showed the Yankees we had a lot more ways of scoring runs than they thought," Irvin said, with a huge smile.

The Yankees came back to win the second game behind the southpaw Lopat, who scattered five hits through nine innings in a 3-1 victory. A pair of rookies locked up on a play of some consequence in the fifth inning. Willie Mays hit a fly ball to right center that right fielder Mickey Mantle chased down.

"(Center fielder) DiMaggio had told me before the game," Mantle once told me, "that his legs were really bothering him and I was to catch everything between us. That's why I went after the ball so hard."

An instant before Mantle was to glove the high fly, DiMaggio said, "I got it." Mantle turned his right leg on the outfield grass to slow down his momentum. His baseball cleats got caught in a drainage ditch, and Mantle went down hard. He had to be carried off the field and rushed to nearby Lenox Hill Hospital in Manhattan for knee surgery. He never could run as fast as he once had after the accident. Ironically, Mantle's father, Mutt Mantle, was in the same hospital room when Mantle awakened, being treated for leukemia. Mutt died a few months later.

"I didn't realize until that day that he was so ill," recalled Mantle. "He always tried to keep it from me."

The Giants won the third game 6-2 behind the pitching of Jim Hearn to regain a lead in the series. The game turned on one of the most unique plays in World Series history. The

Giants were leading 1-0 into the fifth inning when Eddie Stanky, known as the Walking Man for his propensity for drawing a walk, made it to first on his specialty. Durocher sent Stanky scurrying to second on a hit and run, but the clever Berra, sensing the play, called for a pitch out. Raschi delivered the pitch wide and Yogi fired to second well ahead of Stanky's dusty slide. Rizzuto held his glove hand low with the ball nestled in the pocket as Stanky slid in. Suddenly the ball was somewhere behind shortstop, and Stanky was racing for third. He had kicked the ball out of Rizzuto's glove in what became known as Stanky's famous "dropkick," still in vogue in football. The Yankee shortstop and the Giants second baseman had an antagonistic relationship over that play for many more years. Alvin Dark followed with a hit, and the Giants locked up the game with a five-run inning for the 6-2 victory.

Then came the rains, delaying the series by a day. When play began on October 8 at the Polo Grounds, the Yankees were able to return to their Game 1 starter, Reynolds, on three days' rest. Reynolds was sharper this time around, while Maglie, starting for the Giants and pooped from his late-season heroics, didn't have much. The Yankees collected eight hits and four runs off the The Barber, including DiMaggio's final home run of his career. Reynolds went the distance as the Yankees evened the series with a 6-2 win.

"I think the rainout really turned the series," Irvin recalled more than 55 years later. "If Reynolds had to pitch on short rest in that second start or Stengel had to use another pitcher we would have gone up three games to one. That would have been it. We would have added the Series to that glorious pennant."

Game 5 was marked by McDougald's grand slam in the third inning, which sparked the Yankees to a 13-1 drubbing of the Giants. Lopat pitched a complete game, allowing just an unearned run to notch his second win of the series. With the Yankees now up three games to two, Durocher sent his opening-day pitcher, Koslo, back to the mound to face off against Raschi. Game 6 was the toughest and tightest of all through the first five innings. The score was tied 1-1 when the Yankees loaded the bases in the sixth. Bauer, playing in place of the injured Mickey Mantle, slugged a two-out, bases-clearing triple against the short wall in right field to put the Yankees up 4-1.

The Yankees took that comfortable lead into the ninth inning. Sain, who had relieved Raschi in the seventh inning, opened the final frame by giving up a hit to the Brat, Stanky. Dark then walked and the bases loaded when Whitey Lockman dropped a soft fly ball single to center. Left-hander Bob Kuzava came in to face Irvin, the Giants hottest hitter, with one out.

"I was thinking that if I homered we would win 5-4 just the way we had won the last game of the season in the playoffs against Brooklyn," Irvin recalled.

There was one dramatic change: This game was being played in the cavernous Yankee Stadium instead of the short left- and right-field porches of the Polo Grounds. Irvin hit the left-hander's fastball about 400 feet to the deepest part of the field. Woodling caught the huge fly, but Stanky tagged up to score from third and both runners moved up a base.

That brought up hero Bobby Thomson, who this time hit a ball to left-center rather than down the line as he had a week earlier in the Polo Grounds. The fly ball was again hauled in by Woodling, and another Giants run scored to bring the Giants to within a run. Right-handed batter Sal Yvars was called from the bullpen to bat for the lefty-swinging Hank Thompson. Yvars, who was used by the Giants in the final six weeks of the season as a signalman for the Giants sign-stealing devices, had not batted since August.

"I didn't get along with Leo at all," Yvars later said. "When he didn't use me I let him know I was pretty mad. So he buried me in the bullpen with the sign-stealing stuff and I never got into a game.

"I was always confident against left-handed pitchers. Kuzava threw hard, but I knew I could drive the ball against him. I did."

The count went to 2-2 and Kuzava, not wanting to put the

winning run on base for the Giants, fired a fastball down the middle of the plate. Yvars ripped it.

The ball went on a low line to right field. It clearly seemed to be a hit, possibly for extra bases. Bauer had other ideas. The right fielder cut across the grass at full speed. He saw the ball sinking at the last instant. He sunk with it, sliding on his pants several feet, before gloving the ball just inches above the ground for the final, dramatic out of the series.

"If that goes in," Yvars kidded, "who would have heard of Thomson? I would have been the guy the fans remembered."

Instead, Thomson is remembered for winning the pennant, Yvars is recalled as the man who almost tied up the 1951 World Series, and the Yankees had another championship in six games.

DiMaggio was nearing his 37th birthday when World Series play ended. He retired shortly thereafter, following 13 seasons with the Yankees, a career average of .325, and 361 homers. He finished the '51 regular season with an average of .263, by far the lowest mark of his career. He hit .261 in the World Series that season, but also contributed three extra-base hits and five RBIs. Years later I asked his brother, Tom DiMaggio, why his baseball brother had retired so early. Tom indicated it was because Joe wasn't able to play up to his own standards anymore.

Still, he ended his career up to his standards in one way: with a ninth World Series title in ten tries.

10

1964

A four-game Series sweep by the Chicago White Sox over the Yankees in August, a Horner harmonica, and a needling Mantle combined to set up the surprising 1964 World Series. Before the dust had settled on the 1964 season, rookie Yankee manager Yogi Berra was fired, opposing Series manager Johnny Keane of the Cardinals was the new Yankee skipper, and the vaunted Yankees dynasty was in shambles. The Yankees would not be in a World Series for a dozen years.

Both the Yankees and Cardinals made it to the '64 World Series after breathless pennant races. The Yankees, struggling with injuries most of the year, rallied in September behind an 11-game win streak to pass the White Sox and the Baltimore Orioles. To do so, they had to overcome some team turmoil. After dropping a four-game set to Chicago in August to fall to four and a half games back, infielder Phil Linz, playing regularly in the absence of injured shortstop Tony Kubek, took out his harmonica for some postgame stress relief. Linz was playing "Mary Had a Little Lamb" on the non-air conditioned team bus on the way from the park to the airport. Yankee coach Frank Crosetti ordered Linz to cease and desist. Linz said he hadn't heard the instructions because of the "music" and asked teammate Mantle, seated just behind him, what Crosetti had suggested. "He said to play louder," Mickey replied with a smile. Linz did. Berra, sitting up front, stormed back to the back of the bus and demanded the harmonica. Linz flipped it to him and Berra threw it back in a rage, hitting first baseman Joe Pepitone on the knee to exaggerated howls of pain.

General manager Ralph Houk decided Berra had lost control of the team and would be fired after the season. He also fired famed broadcaster Mel Allen (no relation) in his two worst moves as boss.

The Yankees rallied after the harmonica fiasco and won the pennant by a game over the White Sox. The Cardinals slipped through to the pennant after Philadelphia blew a six-and-a-half-game lead with 12 games to go. The Cardinals had to win the last game of the season after two losses to the downtrodden Mets to lock up the flag. Bob Gibson was the St. Louis relief pitcher on the final day of the season.

Game 1 honors went to Ford for the Yankees and left-hander Ray Sadecki for the Cardinals. The exhausted Gibson was given an extra day's rest. Ford struggled into the sixth but New York held a 4-2 lead thanks to a home run from Tom Tresh and an RBI single from Ford himself. In the bottom of the sixth, a huge homer by Mike Shannon tied the score. Tim McCarver then doubled off Ford to knock him out of the game, and Curt Flood locked up the game for the Cardinals with a long triple to cap St. Louis' four-run inning. Barney Schultz, a 38-year-old knuckleballer, pitched the final three innings to save the opening game, a 9-5 victory for the Redbirds.

Rookie pitcher Mel Stottlemyre, who had joined the Yankees as a 22-year-old in June and compiled a 9-3 record, evened the series at a game apiece for the Yankees with a smooth seven-hitter in an 8-3 Game 2 win. Left hander Curt Simmons, who had probably cost the Phillies a World Series ring in 1950 against the Yankees when he marched off to service in the Korean War, was back as a veteran pitcher for the Cardinals in 1964. He was matched in the third game at the Stadium against young right-hander Jim Bouton, an overachieving smallish competitor known for his ferocious intensity and his flying baseball cap, which tended to fall off after he let loose a pitch. The Yankees got a run off Simmons in the second for a 1-0 lead, but the Cardinals tied it in the fifth when Simmons himself singled off Bouton. The Cardinals tried to win the game in the ninth inning when they sent up slugger Bob Skinner to hit for Simmons with one on and nobody out. Skinner flied out and Bouton retired the next two batters to keep the game tied 1-1 into the bottom of the ninth. Mantle was due to lead off for the Yankees.

"I'm going to hit one out to end it," Mantle told the next batter, Elston Howard, as he strolled to the plate.

Schultz's first knuckleball to Mantle sailed up to the plate about 70 miles an hour and as big as a Halloween pumpkin. Mantle crushed it. The ball landed in the third deck of Yankee Stadium for a 2-1 victory for Bouton and the Yankees.

The Yankees jumped to a 3-0 lead against Sadecki in Game 4 and looked certain to break their World Series slump following two straight losses in 1962 to the Giants and 1963 to the Los Angeles Dodgers. Al Downing, a hard-throwing left-hander, had the Cardinals shut down through five innings. But in the sixth, things fell apart for New York. Carl Warwick singled as a pinch hitter for reliever Roger Craig, Flood followed with another single, and Bobby Richardson muffed Dick Groat's routine ground ball to load the bases for the Cardinals with one out. Ken Boyer dug in at home plate as his younger brother and Yankee third baseman, Clete, moved in a bit at third looking for a ground ball he could turn into a double play.

"I always rooted hard for my brother—but not in *that* spot,"

Clete said. "I wanted him to get a lot of hits in the series, but not with anybody on. He hit the ball out and I had to give him a little smile as he rounded third base."

The grand slam put the Cardinals up 4-3. Ron Taylor, later a relief pitching star with the New York Mets in 1969, shut the Yankees down over the last four innings with no hits, no runs, and a single walk. The 4-3 victory for St. Louis tied the series up and set up a rematch of Game 2 between Gibson and Stottlemyre. The Yankee rookie allowed just two runs in seven innings of work, but Gibson was stingier, holding New York scoreless into the bottom of the ninth. Mantle reached base on an error to lead off the frame, then Tresh sent Gibson's pitch over the wall in right-center to tie the game. Gibson watched from the bench as the Cardinals rallied for three runs in the top of the tenth off McCarver's three-run homer. Gibby took care of the Yankees in the bottom of the tenth to complete the 13-strikeout, 10-inning complete game.

The next day McCarver, who would wind up hitting .478 in the series, had two more hits, and Brock added three of his own. But it would not be enough as the Yankees won 8-3.

"I was just a kid then (25) and every day, every at-bat, every minute of World Series play was a thrill," Brock said in 2006. "This was the Fall Classic. This was the ultimate accolade of the game. Winning. Making it to the World Series. This is the ultimate synergy of team play. Winning, just winning, nothing else matters, no individual accomplishment, no big plays. Just your team winning, being the best.

"The World Series is like a war, gaining territory, gaining status, conquering the enemy, being on top of your profession. You win and then a hundred thousand people in red shirts and red jackets and red socks come out in downtown St. Louis for the victory parade to salute us, their favorites, the St. Louis Cardinals, the Redbirds. There's no thrill in the game that can match that. I feel so sorry for the players who never experience it."

The Bronx Bombers, as was their history and tradition, rallied with power in the sixth game to put Brock's dreams of a World Series parade on hold. Mantle and Maris both hit solo home runs and Joe Pepitone added a grand-slam wallop in the win. Bouton got his second Series win with 8 ⅓ innings of solid pitching. Steve Hamilton finished the game for Bouton.

Both managers, Berra for the Yankees and Keane for the Cardinals, gambled on their seventh-game starters. Berra chose Stottlemyre again, his 22-year-old newcomer, on only two days of rest. Keane did the same with Gibson, 28 years old and in his prime. Both pitchers struggled early, constantly falling behind batters in the count, neither having the overwhelming speed of their fastballs or the bite on their breaking pitches. The Cardinals jumped ahead with three in the fourth inning against Stottlemyre, then three more in the fifth against Downing to give the Cardinals what appeared to be an insurmountable 6-0 lead.

But these were the Yankees. In what turned out to be their last Series gasp in a dozen years, New York battled back with three runs in the sixth on a long home run by Mantle, his 18th and final World Series home run. The Cardinals responded: Boyer added another run for the Redbirds in the seventh to increase the margin to four. Gibson, clearly tiring, held on to the 7-3 lead into the ninth inning. Gibson struck out Tresh to start the inning, then allowed a deep homer to left off the bat of Clete Boyer. The next batter against a tiring Gibson was pinch-hitter Johnny Blanchard, who also struck out. That brought ebullient shortstop Phil Linz, who had triggered the Yankee furor in midsummer with his harmonica version of "Mary Had a Little Lamb," to the plate with two outs.

"All I wanted to do was get on base," Linz recalled. "We were down three runs and if I got on and Richardson got on behind me, then Maris, Mantle, and Howard might win the series for us. Somehow I met the ball and it just kept going. I looked up and it cleared the wall. About 30,000 fans in the stands and I were pretty surprised."

Linz's homer cut the St. Louis margin to 7-5. St. Louis now

had two pitchers warming up in the Cardinals bullpen, as Gibson clearly was out of gas on the mound. Keane stuck with his ace against Richardson, needing just one more out. The smallish infielder already had two hits in the game and 13 in the series.

"All I wanted to do was get on base," Richardson recalled. "Gibson was a great pitcher, but he was clearly running out of steam at that point after all his innings. I figured if I could get a hit or even a walk our big guys, Roger and Mickey, would come through for us."

While St. Louis fans in the stands waited for their manager to rescue his failing future Hall of Famer, Gibson rubbed the ball then squeezed the resin bag behind the mound. Like all great pitchers, Gibson was toughest when the game was in balance.

"I knew I had enough left to get this guy out," Gibson remembered.

The count went to 1-1 and Gibson threw a high fastball just off the plate. Richardson, trying to make contact just to drive the ball into the outfield for a hit, got under Gibson's spinning fastball and popped it up to shortstop Dal Maxvill. The ball spun out to short left field and Maxvill drifted back, camped under the pop up, and squeezed the ball for the final out.

In the St. Louis clubhouse later, the scene was as wild as any that ever transpired in a winning World Series locker room. St. Louis players drank champagne, drenched each other with the bubbly, rubbed shaving cream on each other, and danced to loud music. One of the wilder sights was watching backup catcher Bob Uecker dancing bare foot and nearly naked inside a huge bucket of ice water. The bucket was meant to keep the champagne cold, but it was clearly keeping the catcher hot as he entertained teammates and the press.

Off in a side office, Johnny Keane, who it was later revealed had already agreed to manage the Yankees in 1965, sat quietly as was his manner. Most of the questions from the press were about his surprising decision to keep a tiring Gibson in the game to the end despite a weary arm. When pressed about the move, Keane uttered one of the most telling and touching summaries of a ball player's skill and dedication.

"I had a commitment to his heart," Keane said, his eyes filling with tears.

Gibson, of course, was named World Series Most Valuable Player after tossing 27 innings in three starts. His performance catapulted him to one of the league's elite.

I flew home from St. Louis the next morning and was met at the airport by my wife, Janet. She asked if I had heard the news.

"What news?" I asked.

"Yogi Berra has been fired," she told me.

We immediately drove from John F. Kennedy airport in Long Island to the Montclair, New Jersey, home of Berra. We stopped in front of his spacious classic Tudor home. I knocked on the door.

Yogi invited me in and talked for half an hour about his surprise earlier that day upon being summoned to the Yankee offices in Manhattan, then given the pink slip.

"What will you do now?" I asked.

"Play golf tomorrow like I do every day after the Series is over," he replied.

Soon he would be playing and coaching for the crosstown New York Mets, later managing them, still later returning to manage the Yankees again. When the subject of the 1964 World Series comes up Yogi Berra still has the same answer.

"We shoulda won it," he says.

11

1977

I never saw Babe Ruth play. I knew him only by reputation, as the Sultan of Swat who hit 15 home runs in ten World Series and twice hit three homers in a single Series game. In 1977, Mr. October left Babe in the dust. Reginald Martinez Jackson was the centerpiece of The Bronx Zoo, the Yankees' rowdy team under the leadership of bombastic owner George Steinbrenner and pugnacious manager Billy Martin. Jackson collected four straight Series home runs in four straight official at bats spanning two games. Not even the Babe could do that.

"Four straight homers, five in the series. Impossible to repeat," Jackson concluded years later.

Of the five homers he hit in the 1977 World Series, Jackson is proudest of the one he hit off Elias Sosa, a fastball pitcher who fired a pitch at Jackson's knees at about 95 miles an hour—a ground ball out by most humans.

"A very strong man," Sosa recalled later. "A great long ball hitter. I made my best pitch. I cannot be ashamed. This was not lucky. This was Reggie Jackson. He has done that thing to everybody."

"I overwhelmed that baseball by the sheer force of my will," Jackson recalled.

As typical of any Billy Martin team, the season had featured one controversy after another. Jackson had been signed as a free agent after a season in Baltimore and popped off immediately in a magazine article that *he* was "the straw that stirs the drink"—*not* captain Thurman Munson, the vain and sensitive leader and catcher of the Bronx Bombers. The team was quickly divided into a pro- and anti-Jackson clique. Jackson's lone ally was backup catcher Fran Healy, one of the brighter Yankees, who sided with Jackson, the college-educated star. The other 23 players all sided with Martin and Munson, but the dynamics would change as the season went along.

The Yankees outlasted Boston for the division title and survived a Kansas City threat in the American League Championship Series for their second pennant in a row under Martin. The Dodgers, under manager Tommy Lasorda, ended the Big Red Machine's chances of a World Series three-peat, burying the Reds 10 games back in the N.L. West standings. Los Angeles then took care of Mike Schmidt, Greg Luzinski, Steve Carlton and the Phillies three games to one to clinch the pennant.

Martin made a surprise pick for his opening day pitcher when he selected the left-handed Don Gullett, a former Big Red Machine pitcher and expensive free agent. The Dodgers sent Don Sutton, then a 32-year-old veteran of 12 seasons, out to the mound against the Yankees. The native of Clio, Alabama, always rooted for the Yankees as a youngster.

"This was my ultimate thrill in the game, pitching against the Yankees, the Yankees of Babe Ruth and Lou Gehrig, Joe DiMaggio and Mickey Mantle. I'm standing out there in Yankee Stadium and a lot of those early thrills just came rushing back to me," Sutton said.

Both Sutton and Gullett pitched well in the opener. Both pitchers were gone by the time the game was settled with a 4-3 Yankees win in the 12th inning. Willie Randolph doubled to open the inning, Munson was intentionally walked, and Paul Blair, in the game as a defensive replacement for Reggie Jackson, hit a game-winning single to left after failing to bunt over the runners.

Martin chose Jim "Catfish" Hunter, the very first of the game's expensive free agents, for his Game 2 starter. Hunter was nursing a sore arm and hadn't pitched in more than a month. He lasted only 2 ⅔ innings, gave up three home runs (one each to Ron Cey, Steve Yeager, and Reggie Smith), and saw the Dodgers even the Series with a 6-1 victory as Los Angeles starter Burt Hooton sailed through nine.

After traveling cross country to Los Angeles for the third game, Jackson complained about Martin's use of old pal and former Oakland teammate Catfish Hunter and his bad arm. Hunter appreciated the defense and said of Jackson, "Reggie's a great guy. He'd give you the shirt off his back. Then he'd call a press conference to announce it."

Munson joined the complaining chorus—for entirely different reasons—when he saw the family seats he was given for the Dodgers games in Los Angeles. They were way up in the left-field stands. He threatened not to play unless his seats were improved. No exchanges could be made, however, so the grumpy catcher had even more reason to hate the Dodgers.

Mike Torrez, who would become a lasting answer to a trivia question concerning Yankee shortstop Bucky Dent in the following 1978 season, pitched a strong game to notch New York's second win of the series, a 5-3 decision. The Yankees took a commanding three game-to-one lead after taking Game 4 with a 4-2 victory over sore-armed Dodger lefty Doug Rau. Reggie Jackson hit the first home run of the series off Rick Rhoden in the sixth, while Ron Guidry, emerging finally into the pitcher the Yankees thought they were getting upon signing him, shut

L.A. down with four hits and two runs in nine innings.

The Yankees looked to lock up the World Series in Game 5 with Gullett again starting for New York. The Dodgers smacked the lefty around Dodger Stadium in a 10-4 victory, pounding Gullet for seven runs in four-plus innings. Sutton went the distance for the Dodgers. Jackson hit a meaningless home run in his final at-bat in the eighth inning of the blowout.

The Dodgers had embarrassed the Yankees in 1963 with a four-game sweep behind the incredible pitching of Sandy Koufax, Don Drysdale, Johnny Podres, and reliever Ron Perranoski. Not a Yankee was left from the debacle of 14 years earlier, but the pain lingered for many Yankee fans, who now rejoiced about the opportunity to finish off the Dodgers in Yankee Stadium. Torrez and Hooton were the starting pitchers in the sixth game, with an audience of 56,407 screaming fans in attendance.

The game got off to a rocky start for New York when Steve Garvey hit a two-run triple off Torrez in the first. Chris Chambliss, who had won the pennant for the Yankees a year earlier against Kansas City with a ninth-inning homer, smashed a two-run shot to tie the game, 2-2. The seesaw battle continued as Reggie Smith homered in the top of the third to put Los Angeles up 3-2.

Then Jackson took over, earning his now-famous nickname, Mr. October. Jackson came to bat against Hooton in the fourth with no outs and Munson on first. He felt confident against the Dodgers right hander because Hooton lacked an overpowering fastball. Digging in at the plate, Jackson stared out at Hooton and pumped his black bat several times. Hooton threw a high fastball and Jackson unloaded on the pitch, pulling it deep and far to the right-field stands for his second home run in a row in two official at-bats. (Jackson had walked in the second, his first trip to the plate that game.) The Yankees had a 4-3 lead they would not relinquish.

Jackson had always understood that baseball, especially World Series baseball, was not just bat against ball, athlete against athlete, speed against stamina. It was a good part show business, entertainment for the fans as well as for the fawning media. No one has ever understood that part of the game better than Jackson. His former Oakland teammate, pitcher Darold Knowles, called Jackson a "hot dog," adding, "There isn't enough mustard in America to cover Reggie Jackson."

Jackson took in the glow of his third home run of the series and popped out of the dugout with a wave in the new tradition of baseball curtain calls. In the fifth inning he batted with one on and two outs against Elias Sosa, a Dominican right-hander who threw a tough, sinking fastball. No matter: this home run sailed even deeper into the right-field seats than his shot off Hooton. The Yankees' lead increased to 7-3, with Torrez now settled in and cruising along.

When Jackson came to the plate to lead off the eighth inning the game and the series were no longer in serious doubt. Jackson remained the only show in town. Charlie Hough, a tricky knuckleballer, was the L.A. pitcher. The knuckleball, if thrown correctly with plenty of movement, was as difficult a pitch to hit as there was in the game. It also was probably the least likely pitch to travel more than 400 feet off a bat. A hitter had to supply all the juice because a knuckleball floated to the plate at a pedestrian 65 or 70 miles an hour.

Jackson's previous two smashes had come off fastball pitchers, each on the first pitch from the hurler. Hough figured Jackson would go after his first pitch, so he wanted it dancing wildly as it made its way to the plate. Hough looked in to catcher Steve Yeager, took the knuckleball sign, and stared down at Jackson for an instant. Jackson held the bat back at the plate as the baseball floated toward him. It came in belt-high, flitting into his hitting zone, turning over slightly as it battled the October air. "Room service," Jackson would later describe the pitch. He swung violently and the ball raced on its mission for the straightaway centerfield bleacher seats, kept empty and black so hitters could more easily see the white baseball from their perches at home plate. It crashed into the 20th row of the empty section, immediately bouncing around the concrete steps and coming to a dead stop under a vacant bench. A dozen kids from left and right of the deserted section charged after the ball. As Jackson crossed home plate, landing ceremoniously with both feet, he held three fingers high in the air, etching his name alone in baseball lore with Babe Ruth.

The shellshocked Dodgers got a meaningless run off Torrez in the ninth as the Yankees closed out the series with an 8-4 victory. Martin and Jackson, who had fought all summer in a bitter emotional conflict, hugged for photographers in the postgame celebration. The warmth would last as long as it took to flash the cameras.

New Yorkers celebrated the Yankees victory, their first World Series triumph in 15 seasons, were everywhere. Probably no greater celebration occurred than the scene at 125th Street and Seventh Avenue in Manhattan's Harlem section, the center of New York's black ghetto community. There kids danced into the night.

"Why not?" asked Harlem Congressman Charles Rangel. "Who else do these kids have for heroes—Sammy Davis, Jr.? Of course they love Reggie. He's the black Babe Ruth."

ABOVE: A disappointed Bill Bevens (left) and teammate Joe DiMaggio walk to the Ebbets Field clubhouse following Game 4 of the 1947 World Series. Bevens lost his no-hitter—and the game—with two out in the ninth inning. *AP Images*

BELOW: The Old Professor, Yankees manager Casey Stengel, hugs Hank Bauer (left) after the Yankee outfielder's hitting and fielding gave the Yankees a World Series-clinching win in Game 6 of the 1951 Classic. *AP Images*

ABOVE: Yankee stalwarts (left to right) Phil Rizzuto, Vic Raschi, Allie Reynolds, and Yogi Berra walk off the field after the Yankees beat the Giants 6-2 in Game 4 of the 1951 Series. *AP Images*

BELOW: Bob Kuzava (center) got out of a bases-loaded jam against the Dodgers by inducing Jackie Robinson to pop out to end the seventh inning of Game 7 and help secure another championship in 1952. Youngster Mickey Mantle (left) and Gene Woodling share the glory. *AP Images*

LEFT: In one of the greatest defensive plays of his career, second baseman Billy Martin saves the Yankees with a remarkable catch of Jackie Robinson's Game 7 infield popup in 1952. First baseman Joe Collins (top) arrives late on the scene as pitcher Bob Kuzava (bottom) moves out of Martin's way. *AP Images*

BELOW: World Series ace Whitey Ford (left) and luckless Brooklyn pitcher Don Newcombe wish each other well before the start of the 1955 Series, the only one the Dodgers were ever able to win against their longtime foes, the Bronx Bombers. *AP Images*

ABOVE: The imperfect man who pitched a perfect game, Don Larsen, delivers a pitch in his no-windup style during his Game 5 historic gem against the Dodgers on October 8, 1956. *AP Images*

BELOW: Joe Pepitone made up for his casual, careless ways with this 1964 World Series grand slam against the Cardinals. Teammates Elston Howard (left), Tom Tresh (No. 15), and Mickey Mantle (No. 7), congratulate him at home plate. *AP Images*

ABOVE: Mike Torrez celebrates his Game 3 World Series victory over Tommy John and the Dodgers after the 5-3 triumph in 1977. *AP Images*

BELOW: In one of their few peaceful moments together, manager Billy Martin (left) and slugger Reggie Jackson celebrate Jackson's incredible three-homer performance in the final game of the 1977 Series against Los Angeles. *AP Images*

ABOVE: Catcher Thurman Munson congratulates Ron Guidry after Guidry's splendid complete-game victory in Game 3 of the 1978 World Series against Los Angeles. *AP Images*

ABOVE: Manager Joe Torre celebrates his first World Series title after the Yankees won Game 6 of the 1996 Series over Torre's old team, the Atlanta Braves. *AP Images*

BELOW: Wade Boggs marks his first World Series win in 1996 with a ride around the Stadium on one of the NYPD's mounted police horses. *AP Images*

ABOVE: Reliever Mariano Rivera (center) celebrates with catcher Jorge Posada (left) after the final out of the 1999 World Series, a Yankees sweep over the Atlanta Braves. Giddy third baseman Scott Brosius (right) joins the party. *AP Images*

BELOW: Derek Jeter, the glamour boy of the Yankees' marvelous string of titles after the arrival of manager Joe Torre in 1996, holds up four fingers to signify his fourth championship following the Yankees' defeat of the Mets in the 2000 Series. *AP Images*

12

1961

In over a hundred Yankee seasons, the best team the franchise ever put on the field was the 1961 Yankees. The '61 squad was better than the 1927 Murderers' Row bunch that won 110 games and swept the Pirates in the World Series, better than Casey Stengel's five-straight champions from 1949-1953, better than Joe McCarthy's championship clubs from 1936-1939, and better than Joe Torre's record 114-win 1998 team that turned in with a 22-game divisional lead.

The 109-win club of '61 featured the home-run race between Maris and Mantle with The Babe looking on from above, the best pitcher in baseball with Whitey Ford at 25-4, an incredible bullpen, and maybe the best defense any baseball team has fielded.

"People always talk about the home-run battle as the thing that made us such a great team," rookie manager Ralph Houk once said. "It wasn't that. It was our pitching and defense."

The Yankees endured a tight pennant race into September, when they raced past Detroit and won the pennant by eight games. Maris finished with a record 61 homers, without the help of steroids, and Mantle collected 54 before being slowed down at the end of the season by an infection. Maris' challenge of Ruth's record was simply the most stirring accomplishment of any individual player in a single season in the history of baseball. Period.

Cincinnati skipper Fred Hutchinson brought his powerhouse Reds into the World Series with great optimism about knocking off the haughty Yankees. It didn't work out that way for Frank Robinson and company as the Yankees slugged their way to another triumph with four victories in the five games.

After being skipped over for the opener the year before in 1960 under Stengel's leadership, Ford got the ball for the 1961 opener at Yankee Stadium. Ford had been babied by Stengel as the anchor pitcher of the Yankees, going on four days of rest and often being skipped when the Yankees played the Red Sox in Boston's friendly Fenway Park. Houk had other ideas. In spring training he asked Ford if he wanted to pitch more, especially on three days of rest. The 32-year-old Ford jumped at the chance, then led the league with 39 starts and 283 innings pitched, which just about locked up his Hall of Fame credentials.

"It was just a great season. Everything worked well. I felt strong all year. It was a wonderful experience," Ford recalled years later. "Ralph really knew how to use me."

Ford gave up only two hits and one walk to the Reds in the opener, a 2-0 shutout. The Yankees didn't crush Cincinnati left-handed starter Jim O'Toole, but home runs by Howard and Skowron gave Ford enough of a cushion to bring the victory home.

Joey Jay, famed as the first Little League champion to graduate to the big leagues, allowed the Yankees only four hits in the Reds' 6-2 victory in the second game. Ralph Terry, who had gained World Series immortality the previous year when Bill Mazeroski hit the October Classic's first walkoff homer off him, allowed four runs in seven innings as the Reds tied the series at a game each.

The Yankees jumped ahead to a 2-1 series lead with a 3-2 win in Game 3. Mickey Mantle, who had been battling an infection in his backside for several weeks, played in his first game of the series and went hitless. Maris, who had seemed exhausted at the series' start from his stirring race against the home-run record, finally hit one out of Crosley Field to win the game in the ninth inning after backup catcher Johnny Blanchard connected on a pinch-hit home run to tie the game in the eighth. Luis Arroyo, the left-handed Puerto Rican screwballer, set the Reds down in the ninth inning to lock up the win.

Hutchinson would later describe the Maris home run—the slugger's first hit in the series—as the key blow of the series.

"After that we couldn't bounce back," Hutchinson said.

The fourth game, won behind Ford, was more historic for what didn't happen than what did. Mantle, despite his injury, weakness, and pale complexion, begged Houk to start him again after his labored performance in the third game. Houk agreed but said he would be watching Mantle closely for any sign of fatigue. In the fourth inning Mantle sat on the Yankees bench before the team went to bat. He was bleeding heavily from his abscessed wound, the blood dripping down his pants and collecting on the dugout bench. He said nothing to Houk. He went to bat and singled to left off O'Toole. Several teammates, notably Bobby Richardson and Clete Boyer, noticed the collected blood on the bench and the staining from the blood on Mantle's uniform pants. They walked quickly to Houk, leaning forward on the dugout rail.

"Mickey's really bleeding badly," Richardson said.

Houk called for backup outfielder Hector Lopez. He sent him in to pinch run for Mantle who immediately was moved to the clubhouse for medical treatment. Ford also injured his foot in the sixth inning and had to leave the mound. Jim Coates finished up with four scoreless innings as the Yankees won 7-0 and pulled ahead to a three games-to-one lead.

The great 1961 Yankees team really exploded in the fifth and final game, burying the Reds with 13 runs and 15 hits in a 13-5 win. Frank Robinson homered for Cincinnati, which used eight pitchers in the game, but New York countered with seven extra-base hits, including home runs by Lopez and Blanchard.

The 1961 Series might not have been the most thrilling ever played, but it did put on exhibit the most successful and dramatic Yankees team of all time. Just imagine how good that Series would have been for New York if Mantle was healthy and Maris hadn't endured such a draining regular season.

13

1949

The greatest run of success in baseball history happened between 1949 and 1953, when the Yankees won five straight World Series titles under the guidance of Stengel. The Yankees got into the 1949 Series with a two-game sweep of Ted Williams' Boston Red Sox on the final weekend of the 1949 season, invoking for the first time the mystical Curse of the Bambino. Babe Ruth had been traded to the Yankees from the Red Sox in 1920. Boston would not win another World Series after their 1918 triumph until 2004; meanwhile, the Yankees would start on their streak of 39 pennants in 1921, only a year after Ruth arrived in New York.

The Brooklyn Dodgers, with Jackie Robinson having an MVP season in his third year with the team, had to beat the Phillies on the final day of the season to lock up their second pennant in three seasons and give the team another chance at their first World Series title. The '49 Dodgers featured Roy Campanella at catcher, Gil Hodges at first, Robinson at second, Pee Wee Reese at short, and Duke Snider and Carl Furillo in the outfield. It was a dangerous lineup that had easily outpaced the rest of the National League in runs scored.

The first two games of the 1949 World Series resulted in the exchange of 1-0 shutouts for the only time in Series history with Reynolds of the Yankees beating luckless Don Newcombe in the opener, and the Dodgers' Preacher Roe coming back in the second game with another gem to outlast Raschi. Newcombe and Reynolds exchanged zeros in the opener through eight innings. The Dodgers could only manage two hits off Reynolds and the Yankees managed only four off Newcombe into the ninth. Tommy Henrich, who had been with the Yankees since 1937, lined one of Newcombe's fastballs into the lower right-field stands to lead off the ninth and clinch the 1-0 victory. The guy known as Old Reliable for his clutch hitting was still proud of his accomplishment as he reminisced about the homer in his early 90s.

"I guess I was lucky against the Dodgers," he said in an interview in 2005. "I was the guy at bat in the 1941 Series when Mickey Owen let Hugh Casey's pitch get away from him and we went on to win the game. Then I was able to connect against such a great pitcher as Newcombe."

Henrich was also the team leader when DiMaggio hit in 56 straight games in 1941. Henrich organized a party to celebrate DiMaggio's historic feat, played the piano, led his teammates in a group singing of "He's a Jolly Good Fellow," and purchased a silver tray signed by all the Yankees as a memorable gift for the Yankee Clipper.

"Not that I needed it," Henrich laughed, "but DiMaggio never took me out to dinner in all the years we played together."

The victory made manager Stengel a little giddy in the clubhouse following Game 1, but he knew from his own World Series experiences with the Brooklyn Dodgers in 1916 and the

New York Giants in 1922 and 1923 that things could certainly turn fast. Preacher Roe saw to that the next day when he shut the Yankees down with six hits and made a second-inning run, collected on a double by Robinson and a single by Gil Hodges, stand up for the 1-0 win.

The third game turned into another dramatic pitching battle as Branca faced left-hander Tommy Byrne. The score was tied 1-1 heading into the ninth when the Yankees rallied for three runs against Branca and relief pitcher Jack Banta. New York loaded the bases in the ninth on two walks and a single. With one out, Mize hit a pinch-single off Branca for two runs to give the Yankees a 3-1 lead. A single by Gerry Coleman off Banta made it 4-1.

"I just never had any luck against the Yankees," said Branca, who wore number 13 on his uniform. "I had great stuff that day but we couldn't score a few runs to get me a victory."

The Dodgers, as was their custom, fought back dramatically in the bottom of the ninth when Luis Olmo and Roy Campanella each homered off left-hander Joe Page, who struck out backup catcher Bruce Edwards to ensure the 4-3 win.

After dropping their first game at Ebbets Field, the Dodgers turned to 24-year-old Newcombe, who had gone 17-8 that season to capture the Rookie of the Year award.

"I was kind of overused that year as I was throughout my career," Newcombe said. "I was a big strong guy but there is only so much your arm can take. I lost that opener 1-0 and (Burt) Shotton brought me back on two days of rest for the fourth game. I just didn't have much left."

Newcombe kept the Yankees down for three innings. Then they exploded for three runs in the fourth and knocked the big right-hander out of the box. Joe Hatten, a left-hander, wasn't much help in relief. The Yankees collected three runs off him and coasted into the sixth inning with a 6-0 lead. The Dodgers rallied for four runs in the sixth to make it a competitive 6-4 game, but Stengel went to his pitching horse, the great Reynolds, in the seventh. "The Chief," as Reynolds was called, just fired fastballs and breaking curves at the Brooklyn batters, who went down meekly in order over the final three innings. Let the one-inning closers of today think about that while they count their millions.

With a three games-to-one edge, the Yankees sent Raschi out for the clincher against flame-throwing right-hander Rex Barney. Barney had been with the Dodgers since 1943 and was the pet project of general manager Branch Rickey for a long while. He could throw as hard as anybody Rickey had ever seen (and he had seen Walter Johnson and Lefty Grove), but he couldn't find home plate on most days. Rickey devised a string contraption at the Brooklyn spring training base in Vero Beach, Florida. Barney would shoot at the strings in hopes of gaining better control of that overwhelming heater of his. No such luck. Though he won 15 games in 1948 and pitched a rain-delayed no-hitter against the New York Giants in September of that year, he was still fighting the control battle as he faced the Yankees in the fifth game of the 1949 Series.

He walked six Yankees in 2 ⅔ innings in that final game, allowed five runs, and gave up a home run to DiMaggio. Raschi wasn't terribly sharp in that final game either, with the Dodgers collecting nine hits and six runs off the righty before Page shut Brooklyn down in the final two-plus innings. Page was a big, handsome guy who palled around with DiMaggio but drank a little more than he should have, which resulted in a shorter and less effective career than had been forecast for him. It was in 1949 under Stengel that he peaked in his profession—winning 13 games and saving 27—and his performance in the World Series finale was as good as he had ever been.

Berra remembered Page being as confident a closer as he had ever seen in the game.

"He used to jump over that small railing in the bullpen with his jacket over his left arm and walk rapidly to the mound. The bullpen was way out there in those days and he got there pretty fast. He was one of those guys who just wanted the ball. He had a great fastball and a wicked curve. Nobody could hit him very hard," Berra said.

Reese, who suffered his third straight World Series loss to the Yankees in that 1949 event, saw the difference between the two teams in the bullpen.

"When the Yankees got in pitching trouble they could bring Reynolds back who seemed to always shut us down, or come in with Page who was very tough to hit," Reese once recalled. "We just didn't have any guys like that coming out of our bullpen."

What made the series even more memorable as time went on was the incredible streak the Yankees had begun as the DiMaggio years gave way to the Mantle era.

"Those five Series wins had as much to do with getting me into the Hall of Fame as anything," Rizzuto said.

Ted Williams said the only difference between the winning Yankees and the losing Red Sox in those years of the late 1940s and the early 1950s in the American League was Rizzuto.

"If we had him, the Yankees were chasing us," Williams said.

No less than four Hall of Famers—manager Stengel, catcher Berra, shortstop Rizzuto, and first baseman Mize—established their Cooperstown credentials starting with the 1949 World Series win over Brooklyn. It was truly the beginning of something special in New York.

14

1955

A seven-game World Series loss should hardly be memorable in Yankees lore, but the 1955 Fall Classic, the only championship ever won by the Brooklyn Dodgers, had a lot of reasons for being this high on the list. The last out was recorded by the Yankees' first African-American player, Elston Howard, and it was Stengel's first defeat in the playoffs after five straight World Series victories. An overwhelming burden was lifted from Brooklyn's shoulders as the Dodgers finally beat the Yankees after suffering five frustrating World Series losses dating back to 1941. Brooklyn pitcher Johnny Podres, a left-hander who turned 23 during the Series, won two games, including the seventh-game finale, a 2-0 shutout made possible by one of the most dramatic fielding plays in World Series history.

The Dodgers won a major-league best 98 games, taking the pennant by 13 ½ games over the Milwaukee Braves, while the

Yankees won their sixth pennant in seven seasons under Stengel's masterful leadership. An eight-game win streak in mid-September gave the Yankees a bit of breathing room in a tight race with Cleveland.

The Yankees jumped to a quick two games-to-none lead with victories in Games 1 and 2 at Yankee Stadium. No team had ever won the World Series after losing the first two games at the opponent's park. So the Brooklyn team had its work cut out for it. In a slugging Game 1, Don Newcombe, who could never win a World Series game in five career starts over three seasons, was slapped around by journeyman Joe Collins for two homers. Howard, a rookie, also homered for the Yankees. Carl Furillo and Duke Snider each homered off Ford in the losing cause. Ford always seemed to have enough stuff left for victory even when he was not at his best. In the opener, he received some relief help from Bob Grim.

"Sometimes I think the difference between our two teams was the parks. The Dodgers were accustomed to the small walls of Ebbets Field. A lot of the drives that would go out in Brooklyn were turned into outs when they hit the same drives in the Stadium," Ford said.

Tommy Byrne, a left-hander who collected 16 wins for the Yankees in 1955, pitched a sparkling five-hitter in winning the second game 4-2. Billy Loes, an inconsistent Brooklyn right-hander, who once lost a Series game when he missed a ground ball that he said he lost in the sun, was not up to the challenge in Game 2.

Game 3 was the contest that turned the series. The Dodgers knew they were finished if they fell behind 3-0. Podres had an unimpressive regular season, posting a 9-10 record. He only made the Brooklyn postseason roster after a strong outing the final week of the season following his recovery from an injury.

"In August," Podres recalled, "I was hit by the batting cage. No kidding. The groundskeepers were wheeling the cage back out to the field while I was hitting fungoes around third base. The cage hit me in the leg and I couldn't pitch for a month. The

Dodgers wanted another left-hander and (manager) Walt Alston let me pitch against Pittsburgh in the final week. If I couldn't do it they would use another lefty, Ken Lehman, instead of me."

Alston activated Podres for the World Series and he won the third game of the Classic 8-3. He gave up a home run to a limping Mantle, but scattered seven hits in shutting down the Yankees, mostly with his very effective changeup pitch. The Dodgers hammered Turley and three relievers for 11 hits, including a long homer by catcher Roy Campanella, for the easy victory. Campanella hit another homer the following day, and Gil Hodges and Snider also homered as the Dodgers won 8-5 to even the series at two games each. Clem Labine would earn the victory in relief and Larsen was the losing pitcher after failing to make it through five innings. The fifth game, won on the pitching of Roger Craig, the Brooklyn rookie, and Labine again in relief, put the Dodgers up 3-2 in the series. Two homers by Snider gave Brooklyn the edge in the 5-3 win.

Suddenly, the Yankees were on the verge of defeat as play shifted back across the East River to the Bronx for Game 6, a matchup of Ford and surprise starter Karl Spooner. The young lefty had come to the Dodgers late in the 1954 season and began his career with two back-to-back shutouts. The cry in Brooklyn for the losing 1954 Dodgers was, "We shoulda had Spooner sooner." However, he won only eight games in 1955 before his arm went south and never pitched another big league game after 1955. His World Series outing lasted only one-third of an inning as the Yankees collected five runs in the first for Ford, which is all he needed in the 5-1 victory.

"If I didn't win that game nobody would have ever heard of Johnny Podres," said Ford. "If we lose, Podres never gets to pitch that seventh game with all the fuss."

The seventh game was one of the most remembered games in World Series history. Podres, cocky and confident at 23, boarded the team bus in Brooklyn for the 15-minute ride over to Yankee Stadium.

"How many runs do you need?" asked Snider.

"Just get me one," responded Podres.

Well, the Dodgers actually got him two. A Campanella double and a single by Hodges knocked in one Brooklyn run in the fourth, and a sacrifice fly by Hodges knocked in the second run in the sixth inning. Meanwhile, Podres, who had tantalized the Yankees in the third game with his effective changeup, was firing fastballs this time that numbed the Yankees as they looked for the soft changeup.

"We just wanted to keep them off balance so I threw very few changeups that day," remembered Podres. "Pitching is really all about upsetting the batter's timing."

After the Dodgers scored their second run in the sixth, manager Walt Alston went for the knockout blow. The Dodgers loaded the bases with two out against Grim, pitching in relief of Byrne. Alston sent left-handed hitter George "Shotgun" Shuba up to bat for second baseman Don Zimmer in hopes of opening up a big lead. Shuba hit a hard shot to first base that Skowron smothered for the third out. Alston moved left fielder Jim Gilliam back to his natural position at second base in the bottom of the sixth and sent the speedy Cuban, Sandy Amoros, out to left field in place of Gilliam.

Billy Martin, that tough Yankee rascal, started the inning with a hit. He moved to second when McDougald bunted safely down the third base line for a hit. That brought Berra to the plate with a chance to give the Yankees some hope. He caught an outside pitch and sent it out to deep left field. Amoros, playing far over toward center field for the pull hitter, raced hard to his right.

"I looked up and saw the ball in the air and thought it was an easy out," recalled Podres. "Then I realized Sandy was way out in left center. I thought he was too far away to reach it."

Amoros kept charging at the ball and stuck out his right hand as far as he could reach. The ball plunked into his glove for the out. Both Martin and McDougald, assuming the ball was going to drop for a hit, were racing around the bases, Martin toward home by now and McDougald far past second base.

Amoros recovered his balance quickly and fired to shortstop Pee Wee Reese, standing way out on the left-field grass. Reese rifled the ball to Hodges at first for a crucial double play.

"I still had to get out another tough hitter, Hank Bauer, to close out the inning," Podres recalled.

With Martin back on second and the batter representing the tying run, Podres got Bauer to roll to short for the final out of the inning. The Yankees got a couple of runners on in the eighth inning on singles by Rizzuto and McDougald, but Berra flew out softly to Furillo in right and Bauer struck out to end the threat.

Alston elected to stay with Podres to close out the game. In the top of the ninth, the Dodgers had two on and one out, but Alston let Podres hit for himself and Brooklyn failed to tack on another run. It would be up to Podres to make a two-run lead stick. In the Yankees ninth, Skowron grounded out to Podres to open the frame. Bob Cerv followed with a fly ball out to center field. That brought Howard to the plate with the World Series on the line.

"I had thrown mostly fastballs all game," Podres recalled. "This was the time to show them my changeup again. I went to 1-1 on Howard and then threw a change. He was a little too quick with the bat and caught it down by the middle. The ball rolled to Pee Wee at shortstop."

Reese, who had suffered through all the World Series losses against the Yankees in 1941, 1947, 1949, 1952, and 1953, picked up the ground ball cleanly and threw a dying quail to first base. The ball was sinking as it neared the bag. Hodges, a master magician around the base, leaned forward and caught the ball as it neared the ground. First base umpire Lee Dascoli called the charging Howard out as Hodges leaped into the air. The Dodgers finally had a World Series win against the Yankees. Finally, there would be no cry of "Wait Till Next Year" in Flatbush.

"I leaped off the ground. I thought I would stay in the air forever," Podres recalled.

The Yankees had come within one base hit of taking the

lead in the sixth when Amoros made his miracle catch. This time it was not to be for New York, where the loss was viewed as a small setback on the way to many more titles.

Years later lifelong baseball personality Don Zimmer would kid that he deserved the most credit for Brooklyn's only World Series win.

"If they hadn't taken me out of the game," Zimmer said, "Sandy Amoros couldn't have made that catch and Brooklyn never would have won."

15

1953

Billy Martin made the clutch catch to shut down the Brooklyn Dodgers in the seventh game of the 1952 World Series, then improved on that performance in 1953 with a dozen hits in half a dozen games for an historic Yankees championship, the team's fifth in a row. The 1953 championship put Stengel's first five Yankees teams in a class by themselves.

"I never coulda done it without my players," the baseball wordsmith once said of his October success.

Martin was one such player. The 165-pound second baseman had 64 homers in his 11 big league seasons yet socked five in his five Series appearances for the Yankees from 1951 through 1956. Two of those came in the 1953 Series. Martin batted only .257 in his career, but seemed to save his big hits for big games and was an especially productive October player with a .333 average and 19 RBIs in World Series play.

"I just loved showing off in the Series," Martin said one day in 1977 as he sat in the manager's office at Yankee Stadium, wearing a big cowboy hat and puffing hard on a pipe. "With all the great stars we had on our team it was fun to shine in the Series and make the sportswriters eat their words about me not being good enough to be a regular on the club."

There was always a Gerry Coleman or a Bobby Richardson around to challenge Martin for his second base job, but few Yankees could ever challenge him for his Fall Classic shows.

The Yankees championship was yet another knife in the heart of Brooklyn and its fans.

"I spent a good part of my career trying to get back at them for that one," Brooklyn shortstop and captain Pee Wee Reese once said of the '53 Classic.

Several participants of the first World Series 50 years earlier in 1903, including legendary shortstop Honus Wagner, witnessed the Yankees take Game 1 at Yankee Stadium with a 9-5 victory. Home runs by Hodges, Jim Gilliam, and pinch-hitter George "Shotgun" Shuba kept the Dodgers close, but blasts by Berra and Collins gave the Yankees a working margin. A two-run double by Sain, who picked up the win in relief, and an RBI single by Collins tacked on three insurance runs in the eighth.

Mantle won the second game of the series with a two-run homer as Eddie Lopat, one of the "five timers" to have played on all five championship clubs from 1949–53, outpitched Preacher Roe in a 4-2 victory. Carl Erskine, who gave up four runs in one inning in the opener at the Stadium, came back at Ebbets Field for the third game against Raschi, another of the five timers, in a wonderful pitching matchup. Erskine possessed a wicked curve ball that was as tough to connect with as any pitch by any pitcher in the game. Erskine was on that October day, fanning Mantle and Collins four times each as he registered a World Series record 14 strikeouts. Despite the dominating pitching performance, the game was in doubt until Campanella homered in the bottom of the eighth off Raschi to clinch a 3-2 Dodgers victory.

Future Hall of Famer Johnny Mize sat on the Yankee bench all day bellowing that the Yankees hitters shouldn't swing at Erskine's low curves. "Make him bring it up, make him bring it up," yelled Mize from the dugout to the Yankees, as they struggled against Erskine. Mize finally got his chance at Erskine as a pinch hitter for Raschi in the ninth. He struck out on a low curve. A chorus of Yankees screamed into their gloves, "Make him bring it up, make him bring it up."

The Dodgers tied the series at two games each with a 7-3 win in Game 4. The Yankees blew an opportunity for a big rally in the bottom of the ninth. Trailing 7-2, New York loaded the bases with two outs, then scored a run on a single by Mantle. The always-aggressive Martin didn't stop at third on the single. He charged for home and backup outfielder Don Thompson, playing left field in place of Jackie Robinson, gunned Martin down at the plate for the final out of the game.

The following day, Mantle exploded for a grand slam off Russ "Monk" Meyer, pitching in relief of Podres, in a five-run third inning. Mantle hit Meyer's first pitch over the high screen above the right-field wall in Ebbets Field. A two-run homer by Martin capped a three-run seventh as the Yankee lead grew to 9-2. The slugfest continued as the Dodgers rallied for five runs in the final two innings before surrendering 11-7. Stengel had started journeyman Jim McDonald in the game. He surprisingly lasted into the eighth inning, earning a World Series win to go with his 24 lifetime big league victories.

Back in the Bronx for Game 6, Erskine tried to come back for Brooklyn on two days' rest, but didn't have much left in the tank. He lasted four innings, allowed six hits and three runs, and was relieved by Bob Milliken. The seldom-used Brooklyn right-hander, who had only two big league seasons of service, kept the Yankees scoreless for two innings. Labine took over for Brooklyn in the seventh, his team trailing 3-1. The margin remained the same heading into the top of the ninth inning. With Reynolds on the mound, New York had plenty of confidence. The Dodgers made things interesting when Furillo, winner of the National League batting title in 1953 with a .344 average, slammed a dramatic two-run homer to tie the game 3-3.

"This was the best Brooklyn team we ever had," recalled Dodgers general manager Buzzie Bavasi. "I thought for sure when we tied that game we would win. We had waited a long time for a Series win."

The Yankees would have none of it. Reynolds struck out two batters to send the game to the bottom of the ninth. Hank Bauer led off the inning by drawing a walk against Labine. Berra followed by connecting on a low, outside breaking pitch, hitting a hard line drive to right-center. Furillo, about the best in the business at his defensive position, moved quickly to his right and caught the line drive for the first out of the inning. Mantle then hit a hard ground ball up the middle of the diamond. Reese fielded the ball behind second base but couldn't get much on the throw, which Mantle beat to first.

Bauer was safe at second, Mantle was on first, one man was out, and the batter was Billy the Kid, the bombastic second baseman. Labine knew he had a tough hitter at the plate who was hot in the series with 11 hits. He wanted Martin to hit a ground ball that could be turned into an inning-ending double play. Labine's sinker ball was his best pitch and he specialized in getting out of jams with an ensuing ground ball. Bauer was a strong runner at second and an even stronger slider. If there was a close play at the plate, Martin was sure Bauer would get in safely.

Labine threw a sinker at the knees for a strike and followed up with a high fastball a little off the plate. Labine returned to his speciality, unleashing a sinking fastball that was a little low and off the plate. Martin went down and got the ball with a fast swing and pushed it into short right-center for a base hit. Snider and Furillo raced over to reach the ball after a series of bounces. Their hustle didn't matter. Bauer was a few feet from the plate by now and jumped on the dish with the winning run. Martin was the hero for the Yankees for the second World Series in a row. Stengel hugged Martin in the Yankees clubhouse after the game and shouted to the press, "My boy did it!"

It was probably Stengel's happiest moment in a baseball uniform.

16

1956

The 50th anniversary of Larsen's perfect game in the 1956 World Series was celebrated at Old Timer's Day at Yankee Stadium in 2006, at private parties at Larsen's home in Idaho, and at an impressive New York City banquet.

"I celebrate everything the same way," said Larsen early in 2006 from his home in Hayden Lake. "I'm with a few friends, we have a few drinks, and we have a lot of laughs."

Larsen had his best laugh on October 8, 1956, when he threw the only no-hitter or perfect game in World Series history, a 2-0 win over the Brooklyn Dodgers in the fifth game of the set. Larsen threw just 97 pitches in two hours and six minutes, retired all 27 Brooklyn batters in a row, and ended the game by getting pinch-hitter Dale Mitchell on a called third strike.

"I just took a deep breath and let the last one go, a high, outside fastball," remembered Larsen. "Then I saw (umpire

Babe) Pinelli throw up his right arm at home plate."

"Larsen didn't shake me off once all game." recalled Berra, that day's catcher. "Then for Mitchell, the last batter, we had made up (our minds) that he would shake me off just to confuse the hitter."

Mitchell started his swing at the pitch, then held up as the home plate umpire, finishing his career with that strikeout, called him out.

"By the time he turned around to argue," said Larsen, "everybody was gone. Pinelli was running from home plate into the dugout, Yogi was racing out to jump on me at the mound, and all my teammates were running on the field."

There was a little more pressure than usual on the Yankees as the series began at Ebbets Field. New York had coasted to another pennant that year, but they hadn't won a Series in two seasons with the 1954 pennant loss to Cleveland and the surprising seven-game loss to Brooklyn in the '55 Series. Two seasons without a Series triumph was considered a severe team slump around the Bronx in the 1950s—something that fans of the 21st Century Yankees can certainly understand.

The Dodgers, who had to go to the last day of the season to outlast Milwaukee for the N.L. flag, opened up the Fall Classic with a 6-3 victory behind Sal "The Barber" Maglie, a 39-year-old Mexican League returnee who had pitched a September no-hitter. Maglie had been a Dodger killer when he wore the uniform of the opposing cross-town rival, the New York Giants, in the early 1950s. Now with Brooklyn, The Barber was a key part of a fine Brooklyn staff that included Erskine, Newcombe, Roger Craig, and a pair of unproven youngsters, Sandy Koufax and Don Drysdale.

Brooklyn pounced on Ford early in Game 1, with Jackie Robinson and Gil Hodges homering to push the Dodgers lead to 5-2 after three innings. That was enough run support for Maglie, who struck out ten Yankees and survived a first-inning, two-run homer by Mantle in going the distance. Game 2 pitted luckless Newcombe, a 27-game winner during the season and the first-ever Cy Young Award winner, against Larsen. The result was far from a well-pitched game. Neither starter made it out of the second inning. Newcombe was lifted after giving up a grand slam to Berra, and Larsen fell apart in the second inning after being staked to a 6-0 lead. By the end of the second, Brooklyn had evened the score. Larsen softened his sorrows with a night of drinking with a couple of old newspaper pals, brothers Milton and Arthur Richman.

The Brooklyn bullpen held the Yankees to only two runs the rest of the way as the Dodgers rallied for a 13-8 win. Six New York relievers were used, and only one, Turley, was not charged with a run. The heart of Brooklyn's lineup—Snider, Robinson, and Hodges—combined for seven hits, five walks, seven runs, and seven RBIs.

Down two games to none, the Yankees straightened things out when they returned to the Stadium for the next three games. Ford returned in the third game for a 5-3 victory with Enos Slaughter hitting a three-run homer after singles by Bauer and Berra. Tom Sturdivant tied the series for the Yankees with nine solid innings of work in the fourth game. Mantle hit another homer in the 6-2 win, and Bauer got his first World Series homer off of the 20-year-old Drysdale, pitching in relief. (Koufax sat through his second World Series in a row without a mound appearance.)

Milton and Arthur Richman took Larsen out for dinner on the evening of October 7. Larsen was a candidate to pitch the fifth game but hadn't yet been announced as the starter.

"We drove Larsen back to the Grand Concourse Hotel near Yankee Stadium where he stayed," recalled Arthur Richman, a senior advisor today with the Yankees. "He had a few beers with dinner but he wasn't drunk as the rumors had it. Just before we got to the hotel we passed a church and Larsen said he should give some money to the church. We could see the church was closed so he pulled out twenty dollars and said, 'Give this to your mother for her temple.' We did that."

Larsen arrived early at the Stadium on the Monday of Game

6 and saw a clean baseball in his right shoe. That was the sign placed by Coach Frank Crosetti to indicated the selected starting pitcher for that day. Using his no-windup style, which he started in late August that year, Larsen set the Dodgers down in order—Jim Gilliam, Reese, and Snider—in the first on a pair of strikeouts and a lineout. In the second, Robinson lined out, Hodges went down swinging, and Sandy Amoros popped out. In the third, he dispatched Furillo, Campanella, and Maglie, who was pitching that day for Brooklyn. He was one-third of the way to his perfect game.

As the perfect frames piled up, thanks in part to a great catch by Mantle and a wonderful fielding play by third baseman Andy Carey, Larsen noticed his teammates began to ignore him.

"In the seventh inning I noticed no one on the bench was talking to me," Larsen said. "I sat down next to Mickey and said, 'Hey, have you looked at the scoreboard?' He just made a face and walked away."

Larsen retired Furillo and Campanella easily in the ninth and then faced Mitchell, a lifetime .312 hitter now pinch hitting for Maglie. The Barber had only allowed the Yankees five hits, including a Mantle homer, in his strong effort; yet the Dodgers trailed 2-0. Michell ran the count to 1-2, fouled off a low pitch, and then took the next one. When Pinelli boomed "strike three" it set off a huge roar in the Stadium with 64,519 fans making more noise than the nearby Eighth Avenue subway rumbling into the station.

Larsen had his perfect game and the Yankees regained the series lead as play shifted back to Ebbets Field. Labine was selected to take the mound for Game 6 opposite Turley, who had taught Larsen the no-windup style. Turley kept the Dodgers scoreless through nine innings. Labine was equal to the challenge in his first-ever World Series start. Heading into the tenth, both clubs remained scoreless. Labine retired the Yankees in order in the top of the tenth, and New York stuck with Turley for the bottom half of the inning. Hardly any fan fussed at the idea of a starter working into extra innings in the 1950s.

Labine batted for himself and flied out to lead off the Brooklyn tenth. It was clear that Alston would send Labine back to the mound for the 11th inning if necessary. Gilliam followed with a walk and was bunted to second by Reese. The Yankees chose to walk the left-handed Snider and face the right-handed Robinson. Playing on weary 37-year-old legs, Jackie walked to the plate with the cheers of the crowd in his ears. Robinson took one ball and then lined Turley's next pitch to left field. Slaughter, who had spiked Jackie at first base as a member of the 1947 St. Louis Cardinals, was playing left as a 40-year-old Yankees backup outfielder. Jackie's drive took off as Slaughter charged in. He had misjudged the flight and the distance of Robinson's hit, and as he finally scurried back the ball sailed over his head, crashed against the wall, and bounded away. Gilliam raced home from second with the game's only run to give Brooklyn a tingling 1-0 victory.

It would turn out to be the last hit in Robinson's glorious Hall of Fame career, a game-winning blow over the head of one of his early antagonists. A few months after the season ended, the Dodgers traded Robinson to the hated New York Giants. He soon announced his retirement from the game in a controversial article in *Look Magazine*.

Newcombe was given the starting assignment for Alston's revived team in the final game. New York went with New Jersey native Johnny Kucks. The 23-year-old Kucks, who had won 18 games that season, was on his game as he shut the Dodgers down with a masterful, three-hit performance. He walked three and struck out one.

Newcombe got into trouble in the very first inning when his old nemesis, Berra, drove a low fastball high and hard over the right-field screen for a two-run homer. The ball bounced outside on Bedford Avenue and settled on the nearby garage where the Brooklyn players parked their cars. Berra hit another two-run homer off Newcombe in the third inning, and Howard took him deep to the left-field seats to start the fourth. Alston mercifully went to the mound to take the ball from Newcombe, who had allowed a 5-0 Yankee lead. Newcombe quickly dressed in the Brooklyn clubhouse and crossed over the street to the garage where his red Cadillac automobile was parked. A scuffle ensued between Newcombe and a sarcastic parking lot attendant. Columnist Milton Gross of the *New York Post* followed Newcombe out of the Ebbets Field gates and witnessed the scuffle, which was the lead story in the following day's edition.

In the seventh, the Yankees piled on more runs against Craig when Skowron smacked a grand slam homer into the lower left-field stands.

"That was a pretty satisfying shot for me," recalled Skowron. "I had a tough time convincing Casey I could hit right-handed pitching. He was platooning me then with Joe Collins at first."

Skowron's slam locked up the game for the Yankees and helped close out the Series with a 9-0 win. It was a typical win for the Bronx Bombers with all nine Yankee runs coming as the result of homers.

"We had so many guys who could hit the ball out of the park that we were never concerned about being behind. I think what made us a great team was the threat we had up and down the order," Skowron said.

For the Dodgers, the 1955 defending World Series champions, it was another bitter defeat. They had carried the Yankees to a seventh game again but fell short. Their best pitcher, Newcombe, couldn't get them a win, and all of the team's hitters seemed stymied in key spots by the Yankees' hurlers.

"After winning the year before we had a lot of confidence in the 1956 Series," recalled Snider, who had another strong World Series for Brooklyn with a .304 mark. "I never could figure out why we couldn't beat them more often than we did. A lot of people said it was because Yankee Stadium was a bigger park and a lot of our long flys would be caught there instead of going out as in Brooklyn. Well, the last two games of the '56 Series were played in Brooklyn and we just didn't hit much."

Little did the Dodgers know at the time, but the team had

only one more season of play in Ebbets Field before moving to Los Angeles. There would not be another Series game in Brooklyn.

"I was from California and I should have been happy moving back to Los Angeles," said Snider. "I wasn't. I loved playing in Ebbets Field, I loved the fans there, the excitement, the noise, (loud fan) Hilda Chester—just everything about Brooklyn. I have so many proud and wonderful memories of my days with the Dodgers in Ebbets Field."

Snider came back to New York in 1963 to play with the New York Mets in the Polo Grounds before finishing up his career with the San Francisco Giants in 1964.

"I enjoyed being back in New York and I enjoyed playing in the Polo Grounds again," he said, "but it just wasn't the same. It wasn't Ebbets Field. When I came back with the Mets that's when I really understood what I loved about playing in Brooklyn for the Dodgers. It was all about Ebbets Field."

The Yankees had collected their sixth title in eight seasons. It was a mark that no team would come close to over the next half-century.

17

2000

The Subway Series had become a New York City ritual
between 1947 and 1956, when the Yankees squared off against
the Brooklyn Dodgers on six occasions, and also met the New
York Giants in 1951. The Dodgers and Giants left New York
City after the 1957 season for the golden glow of California.
The Yankees' regular October appearances continued, but
instead of facing a crosstown rival they were playing
Milwaukee, Cincinnati, Pittsburgh, or St. Louis. There were no
more Subway Series until the old tradition was rekindled in
2000 when the New York Yankees and New York Mets of
Queens, New York, met in the World Series.

The Yankees had won in 1998 and 1999, and as the centen-
nial season began it was a goal of manager Joe Torre and the
Yankees to win their third October title in a row. He wanted to
tie the 1972-1974 Oakland A's three straight titles and make a

run at the five-timers, the Yankee champions of 1949-1953. Manager Bobby Valentine, a scrappy former player in the Billy Martin mold and the son-in-law of longtime Brooklyn Dodger historic figure Ralph Branca, brought the Mets their first pennant since 1986. Now the Subway Series would resume in New York City for the first time since 1956.

The Mets had won a World Series in 1969 and another in 1986 in the heated contest against the Boston Red Sox but always somehow seemed to reside in second place in the hearts of New York City baseball fans. A scrappy 2000 team changed much of that, and a World Series win over the Yankees would certainly catapult the Mets back to Big Apple prominence.

It turned out to be only a five-game series, but because of the closeness of the games—three one-run games and a pair of two-run games—and the intensity of the fans filling Yankee Stadium and Shea Stadium, it ranks high in the thriller department. Two left-handers, Al Leiter for the Mets and Andy Pettitte for the Yankees, hooked up in a dazzling pitching duel in the opener at Yankee Stadium before 55,913 emotional fans, many rooting for the Mets and against the Yankees.

"There is something about a Mets game against the Yankees that is very special, very exciting," said Leiter, who had started his career with the Yankees in 1987 and went on to win a championship with the Florida Marlins in 1997. "We played each other in inter-league play, but I never felt the same heat as I did when I went to the mound for the Series opener in 2000."

Leiter allowed only five hits and two runs in seven strong innings for the Mets before a parade of relievers took over the chores. The Yankees trailed by a run heading into the bottom of the ninth, but scored on a Chuck Knoblauch sacrifice fly with the bases loaded. In the 12th inning, Jose Vizcaino knocked in the winning run on a bases-loaded, two-out hit off Turk Wendell, one of the flakiest pitchers in modern times.

Game 2 would be well remembered for a broken bat. Roger Clemens faced Mike Hampton, the short, stocky Mets left-hander. Clemens had faced the Mets in one inter-league game that season and made it notable, especially for Mets fans, by beaning catcher Mike Piazza on a high, inside fastball. "Fear," Hall of Fame sportswriter Leonard Koppett once wrote in distinguishing the difference between minor league hitters and those who make it comfortably in the big leagues. Koppett suggested in lyrical literature that it was the conquest of that fear at the plate that allowed hitters to realize their talent and move up the baseball chain. Piazza had surely tamed his fear as he was well on his way to a Hall of Fame career. Still, he stored that midsummer event in his memory bank and was given a reason to tap back into it during Game 2. Facing Clemens, Piazza ran the count to 1-1, then hit a foul ball after a hard swing. The thrust of his follow through shattered the bat, the barrel rolled toward Clemens at the mound. The handle of the bat still remained in Piazza's hands as he jogged toward first base in case the batted ball landed fair.

Clemens angrily picked up the jagged end of the baseball bat and flung it toward the jogging Piazza on the base line. Piazza did a pirouette as the swirling bat landed near him. That angered Piazza, who moved toward Clemens and the mound, accompanied by several of his Mets teammates who had raced on to the field to back him up in this moment of crisis. Cooler heads prevailed and no blows were struck. But a tone was clearly set.

The Yankees won the thriller 6-5, and when it was over both Piazza and Clemens chose the politically correct path by expressing no anger toward each other.

"I didn't even know he was there when I threw the bat across the foul line," Clemens claimed.

"I don't think he was throwing at me when he let the bat go," said Piazza.

And you can buy the Brooklyn Bridge from an old bridge salesman.

The game itself turned out to be a dramatic contest thanks to Piazza and teammate Jay Payton. The Yankees built a solid 6-0 lead heading into the ninth inning. Clemens had allowed the

Mets only two hits in eight innings, but yielded to Jeff Nelson in the ninth. After a lead-off single by Edgardo Alfonzo, Piazza hit a two-run homer off Nelson to give the Mets a boost. Nelson was lifted for Mariano Rivera after allowing another single. Rivera got the Yankees an out but then surrendered a single. One batter later, Payton connected for a three-run shot as the Mets closed to 6-5. That was all they could do, however, as Rivera hung on to close out the victory by striking out Kurt Abbott.

The series moved to Shea for the third game, the first World Series game in Queens since the 1986 Mets defeated the Boston Red Sox. The Yankees and Mets were tied 2-2 into the bottom of the eighth when Benny Agbayani, one of the few big leaguers from Hawaii, crushed an Orlando Hernandez pitch for a long double to left-center. Todd Zeile scored from first on the hit, and the Mets tacked on another run on a sacrifice fly to take a 4-2 lead. Left-hander John Franco, the grizzled Met who had been with the team since 1990, picked up the victory in relief with Armando Benitez earning the save. Journeyman starter Rick Reed allowed the Yankees only two runs in six impressive innings.

Manager Joe Torre used an assortment of pitchers in Game 4 as the Yankees took a commanding three games-to-one lead with the tense 3-2 win. Left-hander Denny Neagle started for the Bronx Bombers and was followed by former Met David Cone, Jeff Nelson, Mike Stanton, and cleanup pitcher Mariano Rivera, who threw two scoreless innings for his first save of the series. The Mets had clearly played well in the loss, but as their history indicated, the Yankees just managed to play a little better in October. It all came down to the fifth game as the Mets struggled to send the series back to the Stadium.

In the series fifth and final game, Pettitte met Al Leiter on the mound for rematch of Game 1. With the score tied 2-2, the Yankees loaded the bases against the tiring Leiter in the top of the ninth with backup infielder Luis Sojo at the plate. He ran the count to 3-2 against Leiter with the home crowd roaring for

the lefty to get out of the jam. Sojo caught a low Leiter breaking ball on the end of the bat and drove it on the ground into
centerfield. The lead run scored and another tallied for the
Yankees on a botched throw from the outfield.

It was up to Rivera to shut down the Mets. He struck out
Darryl Hamilton, pinch-hitting for Franco, to open the inning.
But a walk to Agbayani followed, and he advanced to second as
the Yankees paid him little mind. Alfonzo's fly ball moved
Agbayani to third with two outs. The next hitter was the guy the
Mets would have wished to represent the tying run in the last
inning of the last game of the 2000 Series: Piazza. The slugging
catcher had almost singlehandedly made the Mets into a con-
tending team after joining them in 1998. Piazza ran the count
to 2-2 as the roar of the fans filled the huge oval of Shea
Stadium. He caught the next pitch from Rivera almost perfectly
on the fat part of the bat, driving the baseball on a high line
drive to the centerfield wall, some 410 feet from home plate.
The fans howled as the ball sailed toward the fence. It lost a little steam in the deep outfield and began sinking toward the
warning track before ending up in the glove of Williams. He
dropped to one knee in gracious thanks.

Williams rose to his feet, turned to his right, and hugged
teammate Clay Bellinger on the outfield grass. Other Yankees
teammates rushed to the mound to mug Rivera. One of the first
to arrive was Jeter, who put on another sparkling performance
to win MVP honors. In five games, Jeter batted .409 with two
home runs, two doubles, a triple, and six runs scored.

Several players rushed to the side of a teary manager Joe
Torre, a kid from Brooklyn who won his first Subway Series,
and lifted him high in the air on their shoulders. Yankee owner
George Steinbrenner, watching the final out on television in the
Yankees clubhouse, burst into tears as Williams collected the
final out.

"The Mets gave us everything we could want," said
Steinbrenner, "and it was great for New York."

With the victory, Torre became the third Yankees manager

to record three consecutive World Series titles, joining Joe McCarthy and of course, Casey Stengel.

"It's just thrilling to accomplish all this," Torre said. "These guys played so hard and overcame so many adversities. I'm just so proud of them."

Yankees fans were pretty proud of Torre, also. In just five seasons, he had collected four championships. Only a real spoilsport could moan about the 1997 championship that got away.

18

1957

The dynasty of the Dodgers ended in 1957 with the National League pennant victory of the Milwaukee Braves. The Brooklyn Dodgers had won four of the previous five and seven of the previous 12 pennants. In 1957, though, the Dodgers played their final season at Ebbets Field a finished a sorry third. The Milwaukee Braves, forerunners of baseball expansion after their move to Wisconsin from Boston in 1953, beat out the St. Louis Cardinals for the flag.

Young stars such as Hank Aaron, Eddie Mathews, and Del Crandall, with help from old vets Warren Spahn, Lew Burdette, and Joe Adcock, anchored the Braves to the franchise's first pennant since the 1914 Miracle Braves. The key for the Braves in the World Series was Burdette, who pitched 24 scoreless innings and won three complete games, the first hurler to turn in that trick since Stan Coveleski did it for the Cleveland

Indians against the Dodgers in 1920.

The Yankees were dealing with rumors of the impending retirement of their aging skipper, Stengel. Stories about Stengel sleeping on the bench filtered into the press.

"What about it?" Stengel bellowed when confronted with the player gossip about his dugout naps. "A lot of players my age (67) are dead at the present time."

Things seemed well scripted for Game 1 with future Hall of Fame left-handers Ford and Spahn matching up for a spirited opener.

"If you had one game to win and your life depended on it," Stengel once said of his left-hander, "I would go with Ford."

Stengel's life didn't hang in the balance of Game 1, but Ford pitched like it did, allowing the Braves only five hits in nine innings. Spahn gave the Yankees nine hits, and the Bombers won the opener at the Stadium 3-1.

Burdette, a longtime Yankee farm hand who made it to the big club for a cup of coffee in 1950 before being traded away in a deal for Johnny Sain, started the second game for the Braves against another left-hander, Bobby Shantz. Using an assortment of pitches including an alleged spitter, Burdette shut the Yankees down with only seven hits through nine innings. Hank Bauer did the only serious damage against Burdette with a home run, but a triple by young Aaron and a homer by loquacious Johnny Logan gave the Braves a 4-2 victory as they tied the Series at a game each.

"He was a good pitcher," Berra remembered of Burdette. "He had a lot of different pitches and he could put most of them where he wanted."

A young shortstop from Milwaukee, Tony Kubek, returned home in the enemy uniform of the Yankees for the third game in Milwaukee's County Stadium and celebrated his arrival with two home runs. Kubek's shots led the Yankees to a 12-3 win. Bob Buhl was the victim of the Yankee onslaught that began with three runs in the first inning on Kubek's home run, a couple walks, a sacrifice fly, and a single by Harry "Suitcase"

Simpson, who earned his colorful nickname with five big league clubs, half a dozen minor league teams, and another seven Negro League addresses.

Game 4 turned out to be the most dramatic of the series as Milwaukee edged New York 7-5 to even the Fall Classic at two games each. Aaron and first baseman Frank Torre built a 4-1 lead for Spahn with home runs off Yankees starter Tom Sturdivant. In the ninth, Spahn allowed back-to-back, two-out singles to Berra and McDougald before surrendering a deep home run to Howard on a full-count pitch to tie the game. Milwaukee manager Fred Haney stayed with Spahn, who retired Andy Carey for the final out of the frame. Haney sent Spahn back to the mound for the tenth inning. That certainly looked like a mistake as Kubek beat out an infield hit and Bauer tripled him home for a 5-4 Yankees lead. Spahn then retired Mantle to end the threat.

A stubborn Milwaukee club wasn't done just yet. Vernal "Nippy" Jones batted for Spahn to lead off the bottom of the tenth. Left-hander Tommy Byrne let loose a wild curve ball that may or may not have hit Jones on the foot. Jones jumped around the plate as if severely injured and Haney insisted he be sent to first as a hit batsman. While the heated discussion ensued, Jones strolled a few feet over to the side where the baseball sat in the dirt. He picked up the ball, showed it to home plate umpire Augie Donatelli, and insisted the smudge on the ball was from the shoe polish on his shoes. Donatelli agreed and sent Jones to first base. Felix Mantilla, later to be an historic Met on the losingest team in baseball history, the 1962 Mets, ran for Jones.

Stengel went to his pen and gave the ball to Bob Grim. Red Schoendienst, who had come to the Braves in a July trade with the Giants, bunted Mantilla to second, setting up a key at-bat with Johnny Logan. The veteran shortstop smashed a long double, sending Mantilla home with the tying run for the Braves. The left-handed Mathews delivered the big blow in the next at-bat, taking Grim downtown for a long home run to right to give the Braves a 7-5 triumph.

Burdette was back again as the Milwaukee starter in the fifth game against Ford. Burdette had a crusty face and a mean disposition. The fact that he was facing the Yankees gave him just a little more incentive as he went after his second victory over his former team. After five scoreless innings Mathews beat out a slow roller behind second base for a hit. Aaron then caught one of Ford's curves and dropped it into center field for a single to advance Mathews to second. That brought Adcock to the plate. He had hit only 12 homers in an injury-filled 1957 season, but he was not a batter to be taken lightly by the slick New York lefty. Ford worked the count to 2-2 against Adcock, then threw a low fastball on the outside part of the plate that Adcock slapped into right field for a line-drive single as Mathews raced home with the first and only run of the game.

"He was a real strong batter," Ford recalled of his encounter with Adcock some 50 years prior. "You could make a good pitch on him but he could still muscle the ball into the outfield. That's what happened on that one."

Burdette made the lone run stand up the rest of the way, scattering seven hits and walking no one. The victory gave the Braves a 3-2 advantage and had the team's fans dancing down Wisconsin Avenue.

The sixth game was another thriller with the Bronx Bombers taking the victory in old-fashioned Yankee style with the long ball. Turley faced Buhl in a pitchers' duel. Berra got the Yankees going with a two-run homer in the third, and the Braves tied the game at 2-2 on home runs by Aaron and Torre. In the bottom of the seventh inning, Bauer connected for a homer off Milwaukee reliever Ernie Johnson for a 3-2 New York lead. Turley, who allowed only four hits, shut the Braves down the rest of the way. The victory tied the series at three games each.

Game 7 was supposed to be another outing by Spahn against the only perfect-game pitcher in World Series history, Don Larsen, for the championship. It didn't quite work out that way. Spahn came down with the flu and despite all efforts by the team doctors to push him out there for the seventh game, he couldn't get out of his hotel bed. Haney called Burdette in his hotel room just before the team was boarding the bus for the short ride from their Manhattan hotel to the Bronx ballpark.

"Spahnie's sick," Haney said. "Can you go?"

"You bet," said Burdette.

The enthusiastic Burdette was given the baseball despite shutting the Yankees out just three days earlier in Milwaukee. He showed no signs of strain as he got through the first couple of innings. In the third, the Braves built a cushion with four runs off Larsen and Bobby Shantz. After that it was just a long afternoon of frustration for Stengel's boys with Burdette only strengthening as the game went on. He allowed the Yankees only seven hits, walked one batter, and was toughest when the Yankees managed to get a couple runners on base in the bottom of the ninth. A trio of singles by McDougald, Jerry Coleman, and reliever Tommy Byrne loaded the bases with two outs and New York down 5-0. Burdette got out of the game's lone jam, though, inducing Skowron to ground out to third to end the game. It was Burdette's third victory of the series, his third complete game, and his second straight shutout against the vaunted Bombers.

It would be 11 years, 1968, before another pitcher, Mickey Lolich, would win three World Series games. Burdette was an easy choice for World Series MVP, although he received plenty of help from the young Mathews—who had three doubles, a homer, and walked eight times—and the younger Aaron.

"That was my fourth year in the big leagues," said Aaron, who batted .393 in the series with three home runs. "I think I was starting to learn how to play the game."

It was only the fifth year of big league baseball for Milwaukee after nearly half a century with only a minor-league team. The beer parties went long and loud as the Braves came home to a victory parade.

"It was always a lot of fun to play there," said Frank Torre.

"The fans were very enthusiastic and very supportive of us. It was hard to pay for a suit of clothes in that town or buy a car at the list price."

For the Yankees it was their second World Series loss under Stengel in the last three attempts. Some of the glow surrounding Stengel was beginning to dim.

19

1963

This was the World Series everyone had waited for, a rematch of the Dodgers against the Yankees, except this time it was the Los Angeles Dodgers instead of the Brooklyn Dodgers. After the first two games at Yankee Stadium, the teams traveled west to California for Game 3 at the shiny, new Dodger Stadium in the Chavez Ravine section of Los Angeles. O'Malley never gained permission from New York City's powerful parks commissioner, Robert Moses, to build a baseball stadium in downtown Brooklyn at the Atlantic Avenue intersection of the Long Island railroad. O'Malley had purchased the rights to build a ballpark at Chavez Ravine for a measly buck. That great deal lured the Dodgers west, and New York Giants owner Horace Stoneham followed suit with a move to windy San Francisco.

While the October reunion of the Dodgers and Yankees was the highlight for fans, the first cross-country chartered flight for the working press was the highlight for many of the media. The flight, promoted by the Baseball Writers Association of America, allowed the sportswriters covering the World Series to be on hand for the Friday workout at gorgeous Dodger Stadium. The sun seemed brighter and the grass greener in the new park. That created some jealousies for the New York sportswriters, some of which were also still bitter about the Dodgers' move out west. All signs pointed to a tense series on the field and in the press box.

The New York press promoted the hitting of the Yankees, only two years removed from the dramatic 1961 home-run race of Maris and Mantle. Those two sluggers, along with Howard, Joe Pepitone, and young Tom Tresh, presented a formidable attack that New Yorkers thought certainly would destroy L.A.'s pitching staff. The Los Angeles media wrote about their great arms, led by Sandy Koufax (25-5 with a 1.88 ERA that year), 19-game winner Don Drysdale, and Johnny Podres, the 1955 Brooklyn World Series hero against the Yankees. The Dodgers also had the best reliever in the game, left-hander Ron Perranoski (16 wins and 21 saves) ready in case any of their three starters needed help. The Yankees pitching seemed equally as strong with the gifted Ford still at his pitching peak, two promising youngsters in Jim Bouton and hard-throwing lefty Al Downing, and a decent bullpen led by Hal Reniff. Stengel, the former Yankees manager now leading the New York Mets, was asked about the matchup of the hard-hitting Bombers and the hard-throwing Dodgers. In typical Stengel style, he replied, "Good pitching will stop good hitting every time or vice versa." (Stengel didn't want to commit to a winner. Few experts did.)

It turned out to be a thrilling series with two one-run games and two three-run games, never settled until the final out. In the end, Los Angeles' pitching just seemed to overwhelm the fading Bomber dynasty in this set of October contests.

Koufax, now considered the best pitcher in the game after half a dozen struggling years with the Dodgers, was manager Walt Alston's choice for the opener against Ford at Yankee

Stadium. The kid from Brooklyn was perfectly at home as he opened the series by striking out the first five Yankees he faced—Kubek, Bobby Richardson, Tresh, Mantle, and Maris—in an exhibition almost unequalled in Series play.

"Each pitch he threw me was higher than the one before," Mantle later explained. "I liked the high pitch and he pitched me high and I couldn't handle it. That's when I knew I was in trouble."

With 69,000 fans packed into the Stadium, Koufax's K parade electrified the crowd, some of which were old Brooklyn fans still pulling for the Dodgers. The supposedly weak-hitting Dodgers unloaded early on Ford to give Sandy the cushion he needed. They got four runs in the second inning and another in the third as Koufax, his fastball sizzling and his curve ball snapping, set the Yankees down with relative ease through seven. The Dodgers' offense, meanwhile, made their presence felt in the second inning when big Frank Howard, the powerful Los Angeles right fielder, hit one of the hardest drives in World Series history. Ford threw a fastball on a 1-1 count that Howard drove on a line just over Ford's head.

"I could almost hear it go by but I couldn't see it," Ford recalled.

Second baseman Bobby Richardson, playing Howard straightaway in the middle of the infield, put up his glove but the ball took off over his head.

"I thought I had a chance to catch it, but by the time I could get my glove up it was heading for Mickey in center field," Richardson remembered.

The baseball, now maybe eight feet above the ground, whizzed over Mantle's head in center and crashed 30 feet behind him with a loud thump against the wooden center-field wall some 435 feet from home plate.

"I looked back and it came to Mickey on one bounce," Ford said. "No one ever hit a ball harder and faster off me. Certainly no one hit one that crashed into the wall that was that low."

Koufax was well on his way to breaking the World Series

strikeout record of 14 set against the Yankees by Carl Erskine in 1953. He struck out the side in the fourth for strikeouts seven, eight, and nine. New York loaded the bases with two outs in the fifth, but Koufax buckled down and struck out Hector Lopez to end the inning. His 13th strikeout of the game came against Phil Linz to lead off the eighth, and one batter later Richardson struck out for Koufax's 14th K of the game. The crowd roared as the scoreboard flashed that Koufax had equaled Erskine and needed a single strikeout for World Series strikeout honors.

Tresh gave Yankee fans something else to cheer for as he dug into the batter's box following Richardson's historic strike-out. With Kubek on first, Tresh powered a blast to left field to put the Yankees on the board. But that would be all for New York. Manager Ralph Houk sent the burly Harry Bright up to bat for relief pitcher Steve Hamilton with two out and nobody on in the bottom of the ninth inning. Koufax still had his 14 strikeouts and the fans wanted more. Bright was a classic jour-neyman, never making much of an impact yet hanging on for eight years. Then came his at-bat against Koufax with the Stadium crowd roaring and on its feet.

The first pitch was a strike. Then a ball. Then a foul ball for a 1-2 count. The noise was overwhelming.

"I guess I'm the only guy in baseball to have 60,000 people cheering for me to strike out," Bright later said.

The next pitch was classic Koufax—high, hard, and spin-ning madly. Bright started his right-handed swing chest high. The Koufax fastball was rising to about shoulder high. He missed the pitch by several inches. Koufax had his 15th strike-out, and the Dodgers had their 5-2 opening game win. Harry Bright had his 15 minutes of baseball fame, and for a few sea-sons Koufax held a new World Series record. (Bob Gibson struck out 17 Tigers in a 1968 Series game to establish a new mark.)

"I think it helped me," Bright said years later. "It got me to a lot of card shows. People come up and say, 'Aren't you the guy who . . . ?' Then they want my autograph."

Johnny Podres, the 1955 Brooklyn Series hero, returned to the scene of that crime—as far as Yankees fans were concerned—for the second game at Yankee Stadium. The Dodgers got two quick runs off Al Downing in the first and added another in the fourth when Skowron paid the Yankees back for sending him west after nine productive years in New York. He slugged a home run off the Yankee lefty and opened up a 3-0 lead for Podres. Willie Davis doubled and Tommy Davis tripled off Ralph Terry for the fourth Los Angeles run in the eighth as Podres continued to shut the Yankees down. But Podres ran into trouble in the ninth after retiring Mantle to lead off the frame. Lopez, a solid hitter against left-handed pitchers, cracked a sharp drive to left. Before the ball bounced into the seats for a ground-rule double, manager Walt Alston was at the mound. He sent Podres to the dugout and called in Perranoski from the bullpen.

The lefty reliever gave up a run-scoring hit to Howard, thus ending Podres' scoreless Series streak against the Yankees at 17 ⅓ innings. Perranoski then took care of business as he retired Pepitone and Clete Boyer to seal the 4-1 Los Angeles win.

The Dodgers took off after the game in their team plane, the K.O., named for the wife of Dodgers boss Walter O'Malley. The sportswriters were soon trailing them west in the first rowdy, roaring, cross-country charter flight from New York to Los Angeles. An off day provided the first look at Los Angeles for many of the sportswriters, while the off night saw many of the Easterners parading down Wilshire Boulevard and taking photos of the landmarks of movie stars at Hollywood and Vine.

For the New York scribes, it was a pleasant distraction from the play of the Yankees, who were tortured in Game 3 by the hard-throwing Drsydale, who allowed just three hits and one walk in a sterling, nine-strikeout shutout. For the Yankees, Bouton, who had gone a surprising 21-7 in his sophomore season, allowed only a tainted run in the 1-0 loss for New York. In the first, Bouton walked Jim Gilliam, who advanced to second on a wild pitch and scored when Tommy Davis' grounder hit the mound and then bounced off Richardson's shins at second.

Pepitone, another Brooklyn kid who had survived a high school shooting to make it to the big leagues, gave the Yankees hope in the ninth with two out when he hit a deep line drive to the deepest part of Dodger Stadium's right field. It seemed like the blow might make it to the stands and tie the game. At the final flight it faded a bit, and right fielder Ron Fairly backed up against the wall to pull it in for the final out of the game. That gave the Dodgers a three games-to-none lead.

The Yankees had won six World Series with four-game sweeps but had never suffered the ignominy of a whitewash on the losing side. It would be up to Ford to keep that streak alive. Koufax got the nod for the Dodgers. Frank Howard, who had hit that giant double off the Yankee lefty in the first game, connected again off Ford with a home run that went some 420 feet into the left-center-field stands to break a scoreless tie in the fifth. Koufax nursed the lead into the seventh when Mantle hit a deep home run to tie the game at 1-1.

In the Dodgers' half of the seventh, Gilliam hit a high bounding ball to third base that Clete Boyer fielded, then fired a high, straight throw to first base. Pepitone looked for the baseball and all he could see were the white shirts of the fans behind third base in sunny California. The ball whistled off his glove and flew into the deepest corner of right field. Before Lopez, playing right field in place of the injured Maris, could recover the ball, Gilliam was on third base.

Pepitone was the rookie first baseman who had been the real reason the Yankees decided to move an aging Skowron to Los Angeles. Mickey Mantle, always the team kidder, had reminded Pepitone in spring training that he was the only change in the Yankees' World Series winning lineup of 1962.

"If we don't win this year it's your fault," Mantle needled the kid.

Willie Davis made the Yankees pay for the error, hitting a sacrifice fly to center to score Gilliam for a 2-1 Los Angeles lead. The Yankees had their last gasp against Koufax in the ninth inning when Richardson led off with a single. Alston had Perranoski throwing in the bullpen, but Koufax stayed on the mound. Instead of attempting to overpower Tresh and Mantle, Koufax threw soft curve balls that both hitters stared at for strike three. With two outs Elston Howard dribbled a slow grounder to shortstop Maury Wills, who rushed his low throw to second baseman Dick Tracewski. "Tricksie," as Dick was known, dropped the throw for an error. Now with two on and two outs, Lopez hit a similar slow grounder to Wills. This time the shortstop fielded the ball cleanly and fired a bullet to first base for the game's final out.

It was sweet revenge for many of the old Dodgers who had suffered at the hands of the Yankees in Brooklyn, notably Koufax, Drysdale, Podres, and Gilliam. The Yankees won the pennant again in 1964 but lost that World Series to the St. Louis Cardinals. Many observers suggested that the 1963 sweep by the Dodgers put the Yankees in a slump that took more than a dozen years to recover from before they could get in another World Series in 1976, then win another Series in 1977.

Who did they beat again in 1977? The Los Angeles Dodgers, of course.

20

2003

The Florida Marlins joined the National League as an expansion team in 1993 and five seasons later became the fastest expansion franchise to cross the finish line when they defeated the Cleveland Indians four games to three in the October Classic. Jim Leyland was the manager then and his team captured the championship on an 11th-inning single by shortstop Edgar Renteria.

Six years later in 2003, the Marlins were back in the World Series against Joe Torre's Yankees. The Florida team had been torn down and restructured again under the direction of new owner Jeffrey Loria, a New York City native. Loria brought back retired manager Jack McKeon to run his team on May 11, 2003, and watched him make it to the Series as a wild-card team. The Yankees, meanwhile, had won 101 regular-season games and were attempting to rebound after losing the emotional 2001

World Series to the Diamondbacks then losing in the first round of the 2002 playoffs to the Angels. Against the Marlins, who won 91 regular-season games, the Yankees were back to their accustomed spot as favorites to win the World Series.

Florida was a young team based on the speed of table-setter Juan Pierre, the pitching feistiness of Dontrelle Willis and Josh Beckett, and the settling presence of veterans like receiver Ivan "Pudge" Rodriquez, first baseman Derrek Lee, and third baseman Mike Lowell. The Yankees countered with future Hall of Famers Roger Clemens and closer Mariano Rivera as leading pitchers, new stars in second baseman Alfonso Soriano and Japanese import Hideki Matsui, steady leader Bernie Williams and a one-season rental covered with stardust for one swing, Aaron Boone. It was Boone who delivered the playoff home run against Boston's Tim Wakefield that busted Boston hearts and sent the Yankees to the World Series for the 39th time.

Brad Penny started the first game for McKeon's team against free-wheeling David Wells, the burly left hander who enjoyed the game as much off the field as on. Williams hit a home run in the sixth to bring New York to within one run at 3-2, but the Marlins were able to walk away with Game 1 by the same score as Penny, Willis (pitching in relief), and Ugueth Urbina kept the Yankees at bay.

Things seemed to return to normal for the second game when Pettitte held the Marlins scoreless over the first eight innings. Soriano and Matsui homered for the Yankees, who knocked Florida starter Mark Redman out of the game in the third inning. New York cruised to a 6-1 victory as Pettitte fell just short of a complete game.

"Our pitching was pretty well lined up by then with (Mike) Mussina, Clemens, and Wells set for the next three games," said Torre. "The great thing about baseball is that not everything works on the field the way it seems on paper."

Josh Beckett, a 23-year-old big-game hunter from Spring, Texas, got the nod for Florida in Game 3. The fireballer struck out 10 batters in seven-plus innings, before being relieved by

Willis in the eighth. The Yankees tacked on a second run to a take a 2-1 lead in that inning as Matsui singled home Jeter. The Marlins pen imploded in the ninth, as Williams and Boone both homered in a four-run inning to propel New York to a 6-1 victory that put the team up two games to one.

There always seems to be one game in a World Series that sets the tone for the series. In the 2003 Series it was the emotional fourth game, a 12-inning drama settled when Florida shortstop Alex Gonzalez hit a walk-off home run against troubled Jeff Weaver of the Yankees. What made the game significant was the appearance of Clemens as the starter in what had been hyped as the final big-league game for the pitcher. No one expected at that time that Clemens would emerge the following season in his hometown of Houston, and that his career was far from over. When Clemens struck out Luis Castillo to end the seventh inning of Game 4, Florida fans gave Clemens a standing ovation for his efforts in that game. Clemens left the game trailing 3-1, and the Florida players saluted him from their bench with applause as he dipped into the Yankees dugout. As the roar grew louder and the Florida players grew more animated, Clemens emerged from the dugout with tears in his eyes and a wave of his cap.

"I was just overwhelmed," Clemens said later. "The fans and the players were just so kind. It was a memorable moment for me. I certainly would never forget it."

The Yankees salvaged the game for Clemens when they rallied in the ninth inning to tie it. Ruben Sierra, long an offensive weapon off the bench for the Yankees, hit a two-run triple off Urbina to bring the game to 3-3. The Yankees went to Weaver in the 11th inning and the Marlins brought in Braden Looper, who shut the Yankees down in the final two innings of the game. Weaver got through one frame but then let the game slip away when Gonzalez drove his fastball deep into the left-field seats for a dancing finale to the thrilling contest.

David Wells was the Yankees hope in the fifth game, but he wasn't up to the challenge. Wells didn't last beyond the first inning, however, leaving the game due to back spasms. In the second, the Marlins scored three runs off Jose Contreras, pitching in relief of Wells. They tacked on one in the fourth and two in the fifth to lock up the contest. Jason Giambi hit a home run for the Yankees in the ninth, but it was too little too late as New York went down to a 6-4 defeat.

Game 6 pitted Beckett against Pettitte. After being signed by the Marlins after an outstanding high school pitching career, the 6-foot-5, 220-pound Beckett made it to the Marlins as a regular starter in 2002 with a 6-7 record at the age of 22. He was 9-8 in 2003 for a Marlins team that snuck into the playoffs. Most observers saw Beckett as a coming star with a great deal of poise and confidence and a world of stuff. His fastball was explosive and his breaking pitches were dangerous. Pettitte, of course, had been one of the anchors of the Yankees resurgence under the leadership of Torre and had gone 21-8 in 2003. At 31, he was still Torre's most reliable pitcher and the matchup with Beckett seemed certain to encourage Yankees fans that the World Series was far from over.

Yankees owner George Steinbrenner, getting restless without a title since 2000, was cornered about 45 minutes before the game by sportswriter Jack Curry of the *New York Times*. He asked Steinbrenner for his prediction on Game 6. The Boss, wearing his traditional October uniform of blue blazer, white turtleneck shirt, and dark trousers, answered the question curtly with a statement that sounded as much of a warning as a remark.

"My gut is we better win," the Boss said.

The sixth game began with Pettitte and Beckett matching zeros through four innings. The Marlins broke through in the fifth and sixth for single runs to take a 2-0 lead. Gonzalez scored the first run with a slick slide into home plate, just making it under the tag of catcher Jorge Posada. The Stadium crowd booed the call and Steinbrenner, witnessing the game from his private box high above the field, waved his arms in disgust.

Beckett nursed the lead with solid pitching, great control,

and a biting fastball. He struck out nine Yankees and never showed any signs of faltering despite his appearance on the unusual three days of rest.

"I felt strong, I felt confident, and I knew this was the World Series," Beckett said after the game. "There's plenty of time to be tired and recoup after the series is over."

Beckett clinched the victory by retiring the last nine batters he faced. With two outs in the ninth, he went to a count of 1-1 against Posada and then broke off a fastball on the inside part of the plate, at Posada's hands and moving for his side. As much in defense of his body as in quest of a hit, Posada swung softly at the ball and rolled it down the first-base line. Beckett, hyper and anxious at the mound, raced to his left, picked up the spinning baseball, and with a lunge met Posada at the base line some 30 feet from first base. He tagged the Yankees catcher then raced to the dugout with the winning baseball.

The upstart Florida Marlins, a world champion in only their fifth season in the big leagues, had now done it again with a second World Series title just six years later in their 11th season. Beckett needed only 107 pitches in setting the Yankees down and collecting the 2003 World Series Most Valuable Player award.

"He just overwhelmed us," said a dispirited Torre after it was all over. "He threw hard, hit spots, and had great control of his stuff. We just couldn't get to him."

The Florida Marlins, all of them brash if the truth be told, had inflicted the second World Series loss in three seasons on the proud Yankees. New York fans were left waiting.

21

1981

The 1981 World Series between the Yankees and the hated Dodgers took on elements of drama only fiction writers could imagine. The Boss of the Yankees, Steinbrenner, was allegedly involved in an elevator fight with two recalcitrant fans in a hotel elevator with the only immutable evidence of the event a bandaged left hand worn by the owner after the fifth game. Los Angeles was up three games to two, enough to get any owner angry.

Future Hall of Famer Dave Winfield, playing his only World Series as a Yankee, collected all of one single in six games and was forever labeled "Mr. May" by the Boss in recognition of his stumblebum October. The Yankees, who won only 59 games in that strike-shortened season, led the Dodgers by two games to none in the World Series before falling into a bumbling four-game losing streak.

Remarkably, a relief pitcher named George Frazier, who was inconsequential most of the year with a single loss and only three saves, was credited with losing three of the final four Series games, and set a record for failure and frustration with the most losses by any pitcher in a six-game Series.

Outfielder Rick Monday had homered for Los Angeles in the ninth inning of the fifth and final game of the N.L. Championship Series in Montreal, thus propelling Tommy Lasorda's Dodgers to the Fall Classic for its third meeting in five seasons with the Yankees. Lasorda's counterpart, Bob Lemon, had taken over again as the pinch manager for the Yankees after first-half manager Gene Michael was ousted after one of Steinbrenner's rages.

"I've worked a lot of years for George," Michael, now a scout and advisor for the team, said in the summer of 2006. "It is always better not to be directly in the line of fire as a manager or general manager."

Jerry Reuss, the tall left-hander of the Dodgers, started the first game against Ron Guidry, the thin Yankee left-hander. Bob Watson homered for the Yankees, Steve Yeager homered for the Dodgers, and Guidry, with a little help from Ron Davis and Goose Gossage, won the opener 5-3. Third baseman Graig Nettles, who had turned the 1978 World Series around with his sparkling glove play, repeated his act with a lunging recovery of a sharp grounder hit by Davey Lopes and a leaping catch of a line drive off the bat of Ron Cey.

"Those kind of plays really frustrate a team," Nettles said. "A guy gets good wood on a ball, hits it hard, and winds up with nothing. I know how it feels. It has happened to me many times."

The second game in Yankee Stadium was another masterpiece by Tommy John, who had pitched for the Dodgers against the Yankees in the 1977 and '78 Series and now was tossing for the Yankees. He allowed the Dodgers only four hits in seven innings in the 3-0 victory.

"Every Series win is satisfying," John, now a minor league

pitching coach, said in 2006, "but there was something very special getting back at the Dodgers after they decided I couldn't help them any more."

The teams and the media chartered out from New York to Los Angeles with all signs pointing toward another New York championship. Dave Righetti and Fernando Valenzuela were matched up for the Game 3 in Los Angeles. Valenzuela, the 20-year-old Mexican left-hander built like a fire pump, and Righetti, the 22-year-old handsome lefty from San Jose, California, were unique opponents: It was only the fourth time in the 78-year history of the October Classic that two rookie starting pitchers had faced each other.

Righetti was roughed up and could only make it until the third inning. The Dodgers jumped on Righetti in the very first inning when Lopes doubled and Bill Russell was called safe at first on a bunt single. Cey, aroused by all the talk of how Nettles was the dominant third baseman in baseball, unloaded on one of Righetti's fastballs and drove it into the left-field stands for a 3-0 Los Angeles lead.

Valenzuela, meanwhile, put on one of the grittiest pitching performances in Classic history. He was not at his best but Lasorda stuck with him despite an overwhelming 145 pitches thrown in the game. Valenzuela, caught by television cameras often as he closed his eyes in his pitching motion and looked high in the skies before unloading his pitch, gave up nine hits, two home runs, and walked seven Yankees. New York was without two stars—Nettles, suffering from a jammed left thumb, and Reggie Jackson, who was dealing with sore leg muscles—and the top three batters in the team's order failed to collect a hit. Still, New York jumped ahead 4-3 in the third, before the Dodgers scored two runs off Frazier to take a 5-4 lead in the fifth inning. Valenzuela, with guile and guts and a great grab by Cey on a bunt by Bobby Murcer, shut the Yankees out down the stretch to preserve L.A.'s first victory in the series.

"This is the year of Fernando," enthused manager Lasorda in a giddy Dodger clubhouse after the game was over. "He didn't have good stuff, but it was one of the gutsiest performances I've ever seen. He was like a poker player. He's the best closer I've ever seen, too."

Lasorda admitted that Valenzuela's outing gave him heart-burn.

"We thought of taking him out several times," Lasorda said. "I even came close to pinch hitting for him. If we hadn't gone ahead in the fifth inning he would have been gone. But I'd rather win or lose with Fernando. He's the symbol of this team's ability to survive."

Valenzuela, who was 13-7 with a 2.48 ERA in his first full season in the big leagues, always looked much older on the mound than his advertised 20 years. Some observers suggested Mexican birth certificates have a way of disappearing. (Valenzuela's career ended at the alleged age of 30 in 1991 after one season with the California Angels.)

Game 4 was another wild one—over three and a half hours long and featuring ten pitchers, 27 hits, and 15 runs as the Dodgers held on for an 8-7 victory. Frazier picked up another loss as the Yankees failed to hold 4-0 and 6-3 leads in the marathon contest. Reggie Jackson returned to the lineup and collected his tenth career World Series homer along with two walks, two singles, and a muffed fly ball—a rather typical Mr. October outing. Steve Garvey, the boyish looking Los Angeles first baseman with the slickest hair in the game, collected three hits for the Dodgers.

"It's mad," said Garvey. "You can get caught up in the chaos of a game like this. You have to keep telling yourself to stick to basics, to keep your head. In the end we outstabilized them. Every day brings a whole new set of crises."

Both starting pitchers—Bob Welch for the Dodgers and Rick Reuschel for the Yankees—were ousted early. Frazier was caught for the winning runs and left-hander Steve Howe, later revealed to be on cocaine during the Series, managed the last nine outs for the Dodgers in gaining the victory. The series was tied 2-2 after a couple of wild contests.

The fifth game was a doozy as well. Guidry matched up with Jerry Reuss and the neat game went into the bottom of the seventh with the Yankees holding a 1-0 lead. With Guidry pitching well and the hard-throwing Rich "Goose" Gossage rested in the bullpen, Lemon felt confident of victory.

"I thought we had the guys out there to do it," he said. "I didn't expect what happened to happen."

What happened was a long-ball assault by the Dodgers with Pedro Guerrero and Steve Yeager smashing solo homers back to back off Guidry, who at the time was working on a stylish two-hitter in the seventh. Reuss remained strong in the last two innings, making the one-run lead stand up with a nifty five-hit, nine-inning outing that put the Dodgers ahead three games to two.

Los Angeles only needed one more game for the title, but Lemon was conceding nothing.

"All we need is a two-game winning streak at home," said Lemon. "We've done that before."

All the Yankees needed, other than the two wins, was a quiet trip home from Los Angeles to New York. That didn't happen. Steinbrenner saw to that. The night after his team's third straight loss to the Dodgers in Los Angeles, Steinbrenner appeared in the hotel lobby with a cast over his left hand. He explained that he had walked into an elevator after the game with two inebriated Los Angeles fans. They began riding him for his team's poor play and Steinbrenner said he struck out at one of the burly men. He hit or missed the culprit, as the story changed several times, and injured his hand in the battle.

The event soon became fodder for Yankee humor by players, press, and fans. Steinbrenner to this day has never explained in detail what really happened, so the incident has become a subject for Yankee lore, almost as confusing as whether or not Babe Ruth really called his shot off Charlie Root in the 1932 World Series sweep over the Chicago Cubs. A day of rain in New York was filled with Steinbrenner tales and testimony about the owner's rowdiness as a college kid at Williams

College in Massachusetts.

When the teams finally got back to business three days later for Game 6 at Yankee Stadium, the Yankees sent John to the mound to face Burt Hooton. The Yankees got a run off Hooton in the bottom of the third for a 1-0 lead, but the Dodgers tied it with a run off John in the top of the fourth. The game was shaping up as the kind of pitcher's battle John was familiar with in his long and distinguished career. A strange thing happened on the way to that climax, however, as John disappeared from the game. The Yankees got a couple of runners on base in the bottom of the fourth inning with two out. In the early days of alternate designated hitters in World Series play, John had to bat for himself. He was the next scheduled batter. Lemon sensed an opportunity to score, and he called his pitcher back to the dugout. Instead he called upon Bobby Murcer, one of the league's best pinch hitters, without giving much thought to his faltering bullpen.

With the questioning crowd buzzing as Murcer stood at the plate, Hooton threw a 2-2 fastball. Murcer got good wood on the ball and drove it deep into right center field. At 35, Murcer no longer had the snap in his bat that he had at 25. The fly ball went out nicely to right and faded quickly into the glove of Guerrero for the final out of the inning. It really marked the end of the Yankee chances in 1981 and the end of Lemon's managerial stay with the Yankees.

Believe it or not, Lemon decided on Frazier to enter the game in relief, despite his two previous losses in the series. The Dodgers slammed Frazier for three runs in the fifth inning and added four more in the sixth inning off Ron Davis and Reuschel for an 8-1 lead. Home runs by Guerrero for the Dodgers and Willie Randolph for the Yankees only served as window dressing in the Los Angeles victory.

There was one other base hit of note. Winfield, who had always irritated Steinbrenner with his presence because his agents had beaten Steinbrenner out of some bonus money on signing his ten-year contract, had been hitless throughout the six games. He finally singled. The fans howled and Winfield, getting the joke, asked for the baseball as a souvenir and tipped his hat to the sarcastic roars of the crowd. Steinbrenner, sitting in his mezzanine box, was livid. Steinbrenner blathered to the press later that Winfield was now Mr. May, a guy who could hit early in the season when it hardly mattered but couldn't deliver in the World Series like his other high-priced free agent, Reggie Jackson, forever honored with the complimentary title of Mr. October. (Winfield, by the way, would deliver the winning double in the final game of the 1992 World Series as his Toronto Blue Jays defeated the Atlanta Braves for the championship. Steinbrenner hardly noticed.)

Upon getting the final out of the Series on a Bob Watson fly ball to center, the Dodgers danced on the Yankee Stadium grass, annoying the Boss to no end. The Dodgers continued their celebration in one of the rowdiest demonstrations of clubhouse exuberance. Lasorda hugged every Dodger in sight and even spread his gaiety to visiting members of the media who had buried his team in their tales after the Yankees had won the first two games of the series with hardly a fight.

Steinbrenner was so irritated by the loss that he refused to talk to the press after the game. Instead, he had his public relations director issue a statement of apology.

"We embarrassed the fans of the Yankees, the City of New York, and all the people in our organization with this showing," Steinbrenner said. "You can be certain we will do all we can to improve our product and make the fans of the Yankees proud of us again."

The 1981 World Series loss would put the Yankees in a postseason slump that would keep them out of the Fall Classic for 15 seasons, the longest drought in team history since their first postseason performance against the New York Giants in 1921. The performances of Steinbrenner off the field and Frazier and Winfield on the field would make the 1981 World Series one of the most bitter memories in Yankee history.

The Dodgers, who hadn't won a championship since 1965,

took warm comfort in getting back at their perpetual tormentors.

"It's always great to win a Series," said Lasorda, "but it is even more satisfying to win one for the Dodgers against the Yankees. There had been a long history of the Yankees frustrating the Dodgers all these years. I bleed Dodger blue and the Yankees made me bleed a lot, especially in my early days as a Dodger."

For Lasorda, the revenge was sweet.

22

1976

The 1976 World Series will long be remembered as the Fall Classic managerial debut of Billy Martin and the culmination of the back-to-back triumphs of the Big Red Machine. The Cincinnati Reds, with four future Hall of Famers in manager Sparky Anderson, catcher Johnny Bench, second baseman Joe Morgan, and first baseman Tony Perez (to say nothing of gambling-addicted Pete Rose), became the first National League team to win two World Series in a row since the New York Giants did it to the New York Yankees in 1921-1922.

Cincinnati shut the '76 Yankees down in four straight as the Bombers made their first postseason appearance since the team's loss to the St. Louis Cardinals in 1964, a dozen years of failure and frustration until rescued under the new leadership of Steinbrenner and the field wizardry of Martin. The Yankees went to the last inning of Game 5 of the A.L. Championship

Series against the Kansas City Royals before they could claim their first pennant in more than a decade. First baseman Chris Chambliss, obtained by general manager Gabe Paul in a controversial trade with Cleveland three years earlier, unloaded a ninth-inning homer off reliever Mark Littell for the victory. Chambliss, the son of a Navy chaplain, waited at the plate for several minutes before the start of his at-bat, while the groundskeepers cleared the field of debris hurled by rowdy fans at the conclusion of the scoreless Kansas City turn in the ninth inning.

"I decided after a couple of minutes that I would swing at the first pitch," recalled Chambliss at Old Timers Day in 2006. "I knew Littell would be disturbed by all the noise and the break in the action. I figured he would throw a fastball for a strike to get ahead quickly. That's what he did and I hit it out."

The home run by Chambliss would become legendary for Yankees fans. The big first baseman never could get to home plate in his first go-around the bases because crowds of fans filled the field. It took an escort by uniformed New York City police officers to allow Chambliss to touch the plate several minutes later and make it official: The Yankees had captured the American League 1976 pennant.

Now the Yankees were in their 30th World Series against the Reds, a team many experts considered equal to the 1927 New York Yankees, the measuring stick team for greatness.

"It was just an incredible thrill for me to be on that famous field," manager Sparky Anderson said in 2006. "Here I was, a kid from Bridgewater, South Dakota, who had hit all of .218 in my only big league season as a player with the Phillies. And now I was leading this great team on the field against the famous Yankees of Babe Ruth, Lou Gehrig, Joe DiMaggio, and Mickey Mantle. You could see all those plaques against the wall in center field. What a thrill."

Billy Martin had played in five separate Series as a Yankee infielder, had won the MVP in the 1953 Series against the Dodgers, and was leading his first full season Yankee team as a skipper into the October Classic. This was certainly the dream come true for the rugged, ragged kid from Berkeley, California.

"The Yankees belonged in the World Series," Martin said before the opener. "That's the way it was when I played with the Yankees and that's the way I want it to be as I manage the Yankees."

Martin opened the series at Cincinnati's shiny Riverfront Stadium, the replacement for ancient Crosley Field, with big, right-handed Doyle Alexander in place of weary Catfish Hunter against Cincinnati's lefty flame-thrower, Don Gullett. It was the Cincinnati pitching, average at best, that kept the Reds from truly being classed in baseball history with the 1927 Yankees or any of the other great teams of the past. Morgan started the Reds off with a first-inning home run off Alexander.

"You play the whole season just to get to the Series," Morgan said in 2006. "You can't be overwhelmed by it or nervous or lose your confidence. We had won the year before so we weren't awed by being in it. After a couple of early looks we weren't awed by playing in the famous Yankee Stadium either."

The Yankees tied the score in the second inning when designated hitter Lou Piniella—this was the first World Series allowing the new-fangled rule—hit a double. He was sacrificed to third and scored on a fly ball by Graig Nettles. A triple by Dave Concepcion and a sacrifice by Rose gave the Reds a 2-1 lead in the third inning. Cincinnati iced the game in the seventh when Bench tripled to score George Foster, then scored on a wild pitch by Sparky Lyle, who had just entered the game to relieve Alexander. Gullett had settled in by now with a sparkling performance into the eighth inning and won the game 5-1 with relief help from Pedro Borbon. Gullett had to leave the game when he twisted an ankle, and would be lost for the Series.

Hunter had almost singlehandedly turned the Yankees into contenders after coming over from Oakland as a free agent, winning 40 games in two Bronx seasons. He was given the ball for Game 2. The Reds got to him for three quick runs in the second, with Bench's double being the big blow. New York tied the game with a run in the fourth and two more in the seventh as Hunter got into his groove. Catfish controlled the game into the ninth, when he retired Dave Concepcion and Rose on fly balls. Then speedster Ken Griffey, Sr. bounced a ball to short that Yankee shortstop Fred "Chicken" Stanley (so-called for his lengthy neck) couldn't turn into an out. Stanley's wide throw to first got past Chambliss and rolled to right field. Griffey took second on the error. Morgan, a lefty hitter, was intentionally passed in favor of Perez, an RBI machine for the Reds but a right-handed batter. He lined Hunter's first pitch into left field for the game-winning single as the Reds won 4-3.

The Yankees were down two games to none as the teams flew out of Cincinnati for Game 3 at Yankee Stadium. Martin didn't take well to those second-guessing his decision to intentionally walk Morgan to get to Perez. Tensions increased in the Yankees clubhouse as the team prepared for the third game. Meanwhile, the Reds, with the loquacious Rose and outgoing stars Morgan and Bench, seemed excited but in control as they walked into the remodeled Yankee Stadium for the first time.

"I'm from Oklahoma," Bench recalled. "Mickey Mantle was from Oklahoma. He was my hero, everybody's hero around my area. It was quite a thrill to walk out there where Mickey had played."

The Reds put the pressure on in the fourth inning when they knocked Yankee starter Dock Ellis from the box. With three in the second inning and a Dan Driessen home run in the fourth, Cincinnati built a 4-0 lead. New York responded: Oscar Gamble's run-scoring single put the Yankees on the board in the bottom of the fourth. In the seventh, backup shortstop Jim Mason, who had hit just .180 for the Yankees in 1976, slapped a homer off Reds starter Pat Zachry. Despite the home run, Mason was pinch-hit for his next at-bat in the bottom of the ninth inning. That would be his lone World Series at-bat.

The Reds padded their lead in the following inning with two more runs, and reliever Will McEnaney slammed the door shut on New York. Following the 6-2 defeat, Martin was at his grouchy worst, complaining about the umpires, annoyed at the pitch selection by Ellis, and vowing the Yankees would win the next four in a row. A heavy rain postponed Game 4 by a day. Ed Figueroa started for New York against Gary Nolan. This time, the Yankees struck first with a run in the opening inning on a hit by Munson and a double by Chambliss.

Suddenly, Yankees fans were given hope that a four-game winning streak was possible. Cincinnati punctured that balloon with three in the fourth on an RBI single by Foster and Bench's two-run homer off the left-field foul pole. The Yankees pulled back to within one at 3-2 in the fifth on another RBI single by Munson. When Munson singled again with two outs in the seventh off Nolan, Sparky Anderson returned to his lefty, McEnaney, to put out the fire. The reliever did just that, retiring Chambliss on a ground out to end the inning.

The Reds put the game and the series away in the top of the ninth when they collected four more runs, three of them coming on Bench's second homer of the game, a three-run shot into the lower left-field seats. Martin happened to miss the action as he sat and seethed by himself inside the Yankees clubhouse. Martin had groused about the umpire's strike zone all game. He and home plate umpire Bill Deegan shouted at each other throughout the contest until Martin rolled a baseball on to the field in the ninth inning. First base umpire Bruce Froemming ejected Martin from the game as the senior official on the field.

McEnaney recorded a one-two-three ninth inning to hand the Reds their second straight World Series triumph. A lot more excitement occurred after the 7-2 final game victory for the Reds than during the game. Martin, for one, sat seething on a clubhouse trunk as the press entered the Yankees locker room. He was in tears and seemed on the edge of an emotional breakdown, not untypical of Martin, as he bellowed about the outcome. He blamed the weather, the umpires, and the fans for the four-game sweep.

"I'm embarrassed for this club," he said. "We didn't deserve

MAURY ALLEN

that. We are a better team than that. The Reds got all the breaks. This won't happen again. We'll be a better team next year."

In the press interview room, where winning manager Sparky Anderson sat on the podium, he praised his players for another brilliant performance leading to the team's second title in a row. The heroes of the World Series had been Bench, who batted .533 for the Reds and collected the MVP award, and Munson, who collected a series-best nine hits and batted .529 for the Yankees.

"How would you compare Munson to Bench?" I asked Anderson.

"I wouldn't embarrass anybody else by comparing him to Bench," he replied. "Bench is up there all by himself. He is just the best player in the game."

While he answered the question, Munson, next to be interviewed, stood in a corner of the room. When he heard Sparky's answer, which he took as an insult to his own performance, he stormed out of the room. (Anderson's statement about Bench produced an anger in Munson that rivaled the disgust he felt when compared in the A.L. to his rival, Boston catcher Carlton Fisk.) He was still angry minutes later when several members of the press caught up with him in the Yankees clubhouse.

Munson, nicknamed "Squatty Body" by his kidding teammates for his bulky presence, was humorless and intense. He had advertised his persona early when he joined the Yankees in 1969. At that time, I asked him if he was thrilled at making the Yankees after such a short minor league career. "What took them so long?" was his answer.

Munson had been an exceptional player and leader on the Yankees, but in person he could be a twin of Sesame Street's Oscar the Grouch.

"Thurman isn't moody," said laughing teammate Sparky Lyle. "Moody means that sometimes you smile."

The New York press' World Series stories centered on the reactions of Munson and Martin after all the dust had settled. How was anyone to know that both would be gone, Munson in three years and Martin in 13, after dreadful accidents, a plane crash in Akron, Ohio, with Munson at the controls, and a car crash by Martin in Johnson City, New York, with Martin at the wheel.

The Reds, of course, would be celebrated as one of baseball's most impressive teams. In the summer of 2006, Bench recalled the events following the 1976 postseason.

"I come from a tiny town in Oklahoma called Binger," he said. "Maybe six or seven hundred people or so. I went home and they gave me a parade in my hometown."

There were 600 people in the parade, Bench explained, as he rode in a convertible down the one and only Main Street of Binger. The "Binger Banger," the press dubbed him. His measurements were already being taken for his Hall of Fame bust.

"The parade went down the Main Street and I looked up and realized nobody was watching," Bench explained. "Then I understood. There were about 600 people in Binger and all of them were in the parade. There was nobody in town to watch the parade. We got down to the one big building in town, the cotton gin, and a guy was there to protect the building. He sat on the front steps and he waved to us and the entire parade turned around and went back down again. It was just a huge sea of red, everybody dressed in the Cincinnati Reds colors, everybody yelling and cheering and screaming my name. It was pretty impressive and I remember it like it was yesterday even though it is more than 30 years ago."

Bench's memories of his post-World Series days are in stark contrast to those of Martin and Munson, who were filled with the sort of sour grapes that would continue to haunt them for the rest of their lives. For me, the 1976 World Series was clearly not one of the most thrilling of October Classics on the field, but remains memorable all these years later because of the players involved and the postseason reactions of so many of the participants.

23

1978

The 75th World Series of 1978 may have been the only Fall Classic to be over-shadowed before the first pitch was thrown. It was another brutal six-game World Series between the Yankees and the Los Angeles Dodgers. No matter how thrilling it turned out to be—and it had its breathless moments—the entrance of the Yankees into the Series in the first place gained more attention that October than anything that happened on the field of play.

Billy Martin's champions went into the 1978 season with high hopes for a repeat. By July they looked to be dead in the water. The Boston Red Sox had one of those incredible starts and were 62-28 on July 19 with the Yankees, running in quick-sand, holding slim hope at 48-42 and 14 games back. Martin was feeling plenty of pressure to reverse the team's fortunes. Under such scrutiny, he offered with one of his brutal remarks:

"One's a born liar and the other's convicted," he said about star player Reggie Jackson and his boss, George Steinbrenner. Martin was forced to resign after making the comment. Mild, mellow Bob Lemon, who believed in opening a bottle of beer win or lose after each game, took over the club. He just told his players to play.

Then a strange thing happened. The Yankees started blazing through August and September, and the Red Sox folded their tents. The Yankees were actually in first place by a game on the last day of the season. The Red Sox won and the Yankees lost for a tie, creating the need for a one-game playoff in Boston. One memorable game. One Bucky Bleeping Dent afternoon, as it came to be known in New England. The weak-hitting Yankee shortstop hit a three-run homer in the seventh inning off the Fenway Park screen for a 3-2 Yankee lead against Mike Torrez, who ironically caught the final out for the Yankees title at the end of the 1977 Series. The Yankees got another run before the inning was over, then Jackson homered the following inning for a 5-2 lead. The Red Sox closed to 5-4 before Goose Gossage got Carl Yastrzemski to pop up to end the game with the tying run on third.

Yankee third baseman Graig Nettles was pleading with Gossage as he let the last pitch go to "pop him up, pop him up," in the direction of Yastrzemski at home. As the pop up sailed toward third the needling Nettles bellowed, "But not to me." He caught the ball anyway for the final out.

The Yankees beat Kansas City three games to one in the A.L. Championship Series and headed out to Los Angeles for the Fall Classic. The Dodgers unloaded on New York starter Ed Figueroa in the opening game with home runs by Dusty Baker and Davey Lopes for three quick runs in the second inning, and put the game away with a three-run homer by Lopes in the fourth off reliever Ken Clay.

Tommy John, who would soon change his allegiance from the Dodgers to the Yankees as a 1979 free agent, kept the Yankees scoreless until the seventh when Jackson homered into the distant Dodger Stadium seats. It was Jackson's sixth Series homer in his last four Series games (dating back to 1977), which broke Lou Gehrig's mark of five homers over four games in 1928 and 1932. Terry Forster relieved John in the eighth inning and locked up the easy 11-5 win for Los Angeles.

Game 2 was a lot more fun to watch, especially the very last at-bat. Ron Cey had put the Dodgers up 4-2 with a three-run sixth-inning homer off Catfish Hunter. The Yankees narrowed L.A.'s lead to 4-3 on Jackson's RBI ground out in the seventh. In the ninth, Dent singled to lead off the inning, and Paul Blair walked with one out. Dodgers manager Tommy Lasorda went to his sensational rookie Bob Welch for the win. Welch was throwing baseballs at a hundred miles per hour with regularity, especially when he was pumped up for a relief role. Munson would be his first challenge with the tying on second and the winning run on first for New York. Welch fired one of his heaters at the Yankees catcher and he lined it toward right field. The ball was hit hard and high, but Los Angeles right fielder Reggie Smith collared the drive in front of the Dodger blue wall for the second out.

That brought Jackson, a fastball hitter, to the plate against Welch, with one of the game's best fastballs. Welch threw nothing but 100-miles-per-hour fast balls to the plate. Nothing fancy: no hooks, no changeups, no tricky stuff. Just high heat. The crowd of 55,982 in Dodger Stadium stood and roared with each pitch. Even in the press box, grizzled old sportswriters, used to October drama, were standing behind their typewriters as they peered down on this titanic battle between Welch and Mr. October.The count went to 3-2 after three straight foul balls. The ninth pitch of the at-bat headed for the plate—another high hard one that Jackson swung through for strike three. Game over. Welch pumped his fist in the air. Jackson turned from the plate in anger. The crowd went bananas.

"It was a great at-bat," Jackson said later. "I enjoyed every pitch except the last. He got me on that one. He was better than me today. Let's see what happens next time."

The World Series shifted back to chilly New York for the third game. Ron Guidry gave up eight hits and seven walks in a pitching battle against Don Sutton. Guidry wasn't at his best but Nettles certainly was in the Friday night battle at the Stadium. The Yankees won the game 5-1 because Nettles turned a couple of Los Angeles doubles into outs with a pair of stellar defensive plays over the line at third base. The Yankees had a tradition of incredible third-base performances by the likes of Red Rolfe in the late 1930s, Bobby Brown and Gil McDougald the early 1950s, and Clete Boyer in the late 1950s and early 1960s.

"Every time I put my glove down, a ball seemed to jump into it," Nettles said later. "You not only have to be lucky to be in the right position but you have to be lucky to have guys hit the ball to you there."

The Yankees tied the series at two games each with a 4-3, ten-inning win in the fourth game on a game-winning single by Piniella against Welch. Jackson, who always seemed to be in the midst of everything for the Yankees, added to the drama of the victory by standing his ground. He was on first base in the sixth inning with Munson on second when Piniella hit a sinking liner to shortstop Bill Russell. Russell trapped the ball, stepped on second to force Jackson, and fired to first for what he thought would be an inning-ending double play with Munson unable to tally from third. Jackson simply stood between the ball and Steve Garvey at first. Then he did a little fandango as the throw neared the base. His hip seemed to turn into the baseball, which was soon floating down the right-field line as Munson raced home with the Yankees second run of the game. Lasorda and all the Los Angeles infielders screamed for an interference call but Piniella was ruled safe on first on the Russell error and Munson's run counted.

"I didn't do anything but stand there," said Jackson with a sheepish grin after the game.

Jim Beattie won the fifth game 12-2 when the Yankees exploded for 18 hits off Hooton and two Los Angeles relievers with super sub Denny Doyle, playing for the injured Willie

Randolph and Bucky Dent collecting three hits each. The Yankees pounded 16 singles in the game, and Munson led the way with five RBIs.

In the decisive Game 6, the sore-armed Hunter employed guts and guile to go seven strong innings against the Dodgers before Gossage took over to shut the Dodgers down in the eighth and ninth innings. The most dramatic blow of the game, a relatively easy 7-2 Yankee victory for the title, came in the seventh inning. Welch wasn't as lucky this time around against Jackson, who caught the heater from Welch on the fat part of the bat and drove the pitch 430 feet into the deepest recesses of the stands in right center for a two-run bomb.

The victory ended an amazing comeback by the Yankees, down by 14 games to the Red Sox in late July and now standing on top of the baseball world as the first World Series team to ever bounce back from a two games-to-none deficit by wining the next four in a row. A glowing manager Bob Lemon, beer in hand and champagne running down from his balding pate, complimented his warriors by saying, "They can sure as hell play."

24

1999

Joe Torre had a long history with the Braves. He was signed by the old Milwaukee Braves in 1960, took over the team's regular catching job as a chubby catcher in 1961, and anchored the club behind the plate until dealt away to the Cardinals in 1969. Thirteen years later, in 1982, he took over his old Braves team as its skipper. He was good enough to be named Manager of the Year. But Torre was dumped in Atlanta after three seasons and carried a good share of anger with him when he matched up as Yankees skipper against his old club in 1996. His Yankees beat the Braves in that October Classic four games to two.

"The idea is to get on that managerial wheel," Torre explained one day. "Once you are a manager the wheel spins around when you are fired and somebody else picks you up. That's how I got to New York."

Orlando Hernandez took a different path to New York. Just

three years removed from his escape from Cuba by boat, Hernandez was the Yankees starter in the World Series opener against Greg Maddux, who made up for a lack of speed on his pitches with impeccable control.

"When you face Maddux you have wonderful swings," Torre explained. "Then you look up and you are oh for four against him again."

"El Duque" Hernandez had acquired every pitch in the book in his years as the pitching star of Fidel Castro's national team. His windup was puzzling and his experience made him a very tough pitcher, especially in October games. On October 23, 1999, he was at his very best in Atlanta. He allowed the Braves only two hits in seven innings, and with relief help from the Yankees' exquisite bullpen, New York shut down the Braves 4-1. Maddux was almost as good as he nursed a 1-0 lead into the eighth. With clutch hits by Scott Brosius, Derek Jeter, and Paul O'Neill and some sloppy fielding by the Braves, New York scored four in the top of the eighth to bring more warm smiles to Torre's face.

David Cone, identified as baseball's hired gun because he moved around via free agency to the highest bidder, put on another of his classic postseason performances in the second game. Cone pitched seven scoreless innings before turning the game over to the bullpen, while the Yankees clubbed overrated rookie Kevin Millwood for five runs in two-plus innings. The Yankees won the contest 7-2, then flew back to New York for Game 3 at Yankee Stadium.

Tom Glavine, the Braves' ace lefthander, pitched seven strong innings in Game 3 despite recently succumbing to a flu bug. Heading into the bottom of the eighth, his team led 5-3. Joe Girardi, more significant for his defensive skills behind the plate and the leadership he offered the team than his offensive skills, led off the eighth with a single to right field. Braves manager Bobby Cox stayed with his veteran against Chuck Knoblauch, who despite his fielding woes could still handle the bat. Glavine, a control specialist like his cohort Maddux, got one pitch up a little high and Knoblauch drove it into the seats for a game-tying home run. New York carried its newfound momentum into extra innings, where Chad Curtis drilled his second solo home run—this one off Mike Remlinger—to give the Yankees the 6-5 win.

That put the Yankees one win away from a record-setting two World Series sweeps in a row, and 12 straight victories dating back to the 1996 Series when they rallied from two games down to sweep the next four against Torre's favorite losers, the Atlanta Braves. Roger Clemens was the Yankees starter in Game 4. He had become a Yankee that spring for one reason and one reason alone: to help pitch the Yankees to another championship. That's precisely what Clemens did in blanking Atlanta for seven innings before allowing a run in the eighth. Mariano Rivera took over and that was the end of Atlanta's chances. The Braves fell 4-1. With his second save of the series to go along with a victory, Rivera was an easy choice for World Series MVP.

"All year they said this team wasn't as good as last year's team (125-50) but the only thing that mattered was winning," said Torre. "This bunch certainly showed how good they were."

Torre had left the team in March with prostate cancer. He missed the first 36 games, managed by pal Don Zimmer, and returned to his job on May 18. With restored health and a World Series triumph, Torre put the finishing touches on his fourth season in pinstripes.

Several Yankees were also dealing with strong, bittersweet emotions as the Yankees swarmed Rivera on the mound following the final out. O'Neill, one of the longtime leaders of the club, had learned only earlier that day that his father had succumbed to cancer. Charles O'Neill had worked hard to develop his son as a baseball player. Scott Brosius and Luis Sojo had also lost their fathers during the 1999 season. Two other significant Yankees had also passed away that season, and their deaths had been marked by black armbands on the Yankee jersey. Joe DiMaggio had died in March after a long illness and Catfish Hunter had passed away in August as a result of amyotrophic lateral sclerosis, the so-called Lou Gehrig's Disease.

The losses resonated with the team. "We're all family here," Brosius said in summing up the Yankees season of personal loss and professional gain. It was probably the manager who summed up the scene best in a joyous clubhouse several minutes after the last out was recorded.

"It's your work, it's your profession, it's your hobby," Torre said of the game of baseball, "but it isn't your life. A lot of other things go into that."

25

1998

Ted Williams hit .200 in his only World Series in 1946. Stan Musial hit .256 in his four World Series appearances. Willie Mays batted .239 in his four trips to the Fall Classic. Mickey Mantle batted .257 in 12 October appearances and teammate Yogi Berra got his average up to .274 in his 14 times in the Series.

On the other hand, Pepper Martin in 1931, Johnny Lindell in 1947, and Phil Garner in 1971 each batted .500 in seven games in their World Series appearances. Mickey Hatcher of the Cincinnati Reds batted .750 in four games in 1990, Joe Gordon of the Yankees batted .500 in five games in 1941, and Billy Martin of the Yankees did the same in six games in 1953.

The San Diego Padres' first Hall of Famer, Tony Gwynn, hit .500 for the San Diego Padres in the team's only World Series appearance in 1998. Gwynn, an eight-time National League batting champion with a .338 career mark, also clubbed a homer and collected three RBIs in the series—none of which altered the outcome for the Padres, who were swept in four games by New York. San Diego was overmatched from beginning to end, clearly earning this Series the title of most boring, lackluster Yankees Series win in the 39 Fall Classics the Yankees have been involved in and the 26 titles they have won.

It wasn't that the Padres were such a bad ball club. It was more that the Yankees were an incredible team that year with 114 regular-season victories for an amazing 22-game edge for the division title. New York then swept the Texas Rangers in the Division Series and enjoyed a come-from-behind four games-to-two triumph over the talented Cleveland Indians in the Championship Series. The astounding 114-win total guaranteed the Yankees the position as strong favorites as the 1998 World Series opened on October 17 in Yankee Stadium.

Kevin Brown, one of baseball's most unpleasant grumps, opened for the Padres against David Wells, who lived only a few minutes from downtown Qualcomm Stadium in San Diego.

"I rooted for the Padres as a kid," said Wells, "but then I got signed by the Blue Jays and my loyalties shifted to the teams I was playing with."

Wells, who was now proud of his Yankee status, had enjoyed a fine season: 18-4 with a 3.49 ERA. A seven-run seventh inning by the Yankees bailed out Wells, who had surrendered five runs himself. The Yankees had softened up Brown in the second inning when Chili Davis crashed a line drive off the left shin of the San Diego starter. Brown toughed it out into the seventh inning before the pain damaged his motion. Wells, meanwhile, survived two homers by Greg Vaughn and another by the classy Gwynn to collect the 9-6 victory.

"I think we just had a better, deeper club," said Tino Martinez, whose grand slam capped the big seventh inning. "Even when we were behind early in that game nobody on this club thought we were in trouble. This was a team that could always score late and often."

Orlando Hernandez allowed the Padres only one run through seven innings in the second game. The Yankees rattled the Padres staff for 16 hits, including homers by Bernie Williams and Jorge Posada, and put another nine runs up on the Stadium scoreboard in jumping to a two game-to-none lead with the 9-3 victory.

David Cone, as tough a pitcher and competitor as ever wore a Yankee uniform, was the anchor for the Yankees' third-game victory. He kept the Padres scoreless through five innings as he matched zips with former Yankee Sterling Hitchcock. The Padres jumped on Cone for three runs in the sixth, but New York responded to regain the lead following a long homer by Brosius in the seventh and another shot by Brosius in the eighth, this time a three-run blast off Trevor Hoffman. That gave the Yankees a 5-3 lead heading into the bottom of the eighth. San Diego picked up a run to close the score to 5-4, but then Rivera shut the Padres down for the 5-4 triumph.

Now the Yankees were just a game away from the team's seventh World Series sweep. They gave the ball to Andy Pettitte, who had been struggling with arm problems most of the season (16-11, 4.24 ERA) but now seemed ready for the challenge of closing out the series for the Bronx Bombers.

"If he's sound," said an uncertain Joe Torre before the final game, "he's as good as we got."

Pettitte was facing Brown, who was determined to make up for his opening-game problems with a strong showing. This time he was up to the chore. Brown allowed the Yankees only three runs in eight solid innings of pitching. Unfortunately for him and fortunately for the Yankees, Pettitte shook off all the wear and tear of the long, difficult season and turned in his best performance of 1998. He allowed the Padres only six hits over seven innings before turning over the pitching chores to Jeff Nelson and Rivera, who closed out the eighth and retired the Padres easily in the ninth to lock up the Yankees 24th Series victory and the second in three years under the leadership of Torre. The sweep gave the Yankees 125 wins on the entire season, the most triumphs of any team in the game's history.

"That club really became the standard of Yankee excellence," said Torre. "There may have been Yankee teams with better players, more Hall of Famers, but I don't think there ever was a team that had all 25 guys contribute to the success the way that team did."

The Yankees had rebounded from the disappointment of losing in the opening round of the 1997 playoffs. They did so with the usual well-balanced attack. Ricky Ledee (.600 average and four RBIs), Scott Brosius (.471 average and six RBIs), and Tino Martinez (.385 average) were the hitting stars for the Yankees with Pettitte, Hernandez, and Rivera, who earned three saves in the four games, as the leading moundsmen.

It was a World Series lacking in drama, however, as the Yankees jumped out to a quick lead in games and never looked back. There was a sense on the field and in the stands that a hot team like the 1998 Yankees wouldn't have much trouble putting away the Padres. That's the reason the 1998 World Series, of the 25 considered from 1947 through 2003 for this book, earns its ranking as the least competitive and dullest of October Classics.

But it was still the Fall Classic, and a bad World Series by Yankee standards is still better than not having the opportunity at all. Just ask the Yankees, who for four years and counting have not made it to the Fall Classic, left only to mutter under their collective breath, "Wait 'til next year."

Epilogue

by Bruce Markusen

2009 World Series
New York Yankees vs. Philadelphia Phillies

Every successful world championship run consists of a series of crucial moments and accomplishments. Without even one of those moments, a championship can be delayed, if not completely denied. The 2009 postseason provided more evidence of this theory. Without three errors by the Los Angeles Angels in Game One of the American League Championship Series, without Alex Rodriguez's game-tying home run in the 11th inning of Game Two, or without Johnny Damon's clutch two-run single in a decisive Game Six, who knows what might have happened? It might have been the Angels of Mike Scioscia raising the American League flag, and not the New York Yankees of Joe Girardi, the successor to the legendary Joe Torre.

Although the Yankees had won 10 more games in the regular season than the defending World Champion Philadelphia Phillies, they hardly looked like overwhelming favorites to win the World Series. With a pitching staff headlined by Yankee killer Cliff Lee, and buttressed by talented young left-hander Cole Hamels, the Phillies appeared to have the kind of southpaw pitching that could lock down a lineup featuring tough lefty batters like Johnny Damon, Robinson Cano, and Hideki Matsui. In the meantime, the Yankees had additional concerns over the whisper-thin nature of their starting rotation. The lack of depth motivated Girardi to use a three-man rotation, including the enigmatic A.J. Burnett.

Based on the results of the first game of the World Series, the Yankees did not appear destined to win their 27th world championship. From start to finish, Cliff Lee reigned supreme as the story of Game One. Featuring his patented spiked curveball, Lee shut down the Yankees completely over the first eight innings. In the meantime, the Phillies built up a 6-0 lead on Chase Utley's two home runs against CC Sabathia, followed by four more runs against a parade of ineffective relievers.

In the ninth inning, Lee allowed a meaningless run—and an unearned run at that—which served only to prevent him from recording a shutout. Hardly anybody in Philadelphia could have cared about that triviality. Lee struck out 10 Yankees as part of a 6-1 victory over Sabathia, his staff ace counterpart with the Yankees. Not only had the Phillies taken away home field advantage from the American League champions, but they also seemed like clear-cut favorites to win another World Series. A few particularly optimistic fans in Philadelphia started to whisper about the Phillies winning the Series easily — in four, or at the outside, five games.

After Game One, Lee faced questions from the media in the World Series .interview room. A reporter asked Lee if it were true that he felt no nerves pitching a World Series game at Yankee Stadium. "Not nervous at all," Lee said assuredly. "It's been a long time since I've been nervous playing this game. It's what I've been doing my whole life…You do everything you need to prepare, and I try not to leave anything to chance. So what's the point in being nervous?"

If anyone should have felt nervous in the aftermath of Game One, it was the Yankees, who had fallen despite having their best starter on the mound. Having lost the first game at their home park, the new Yankee Stadium, the New Yorkers faced the prospect of a near must-win scenario in Game Two.

Girardi made two lineup changes for the second game. He benched slumping Nick Swisher, putting versatile utility man Jerry Hairston, Jr. in right field. Girardi also sat down starting catcher Jorge Posada, replacing him with backup Jose Molina. The latter move represented a continuation of Girardi's practice of having Molina serve as A.J. Burnett's personal catcher. The least reliable of New York's three postseason starters, Burnett faced off against longtime Yankee rival Pedro Martinez. Formerly a nemesis with the hated Boston Red Sox, Martinez had signed with Philly in mid-season.

This was clearly not the same Martinez who had once headlined the Red Sox's rotation. He no longer had the explosive fastball or the fading power changeup that had made him a Hall of Fame-caliber pitcher. The Yankees broke through against the aging right-hander, as Mark Teixeira hit a game-tying solo home run in the fourth inning and Hideki Matsui added a solo home run of his own in the sixth. The Yankees tacked on a third run against Martinez on Jorge Posada's line drive RBI single, which capped off a rally started by Hairston's leadoff single an inning later.

The three runs proved plentiful for Burnett. Surprising many of the skeptical fans at the new Yankee Stadium, Burnett kept the power-packed Phillies in check. Throwing a vicious curveball and a lively fastball, he allowed only four hits and logged seven strong innings. Burnett handed a 3-1 lead to Mariano Rivera in the eighth.

With Rivera rested and a day off looming, Girardi felt no hesitation in asking his closer to pitch two full innings. Rivera ran into a bit of trouble in the eighth, allowing a walk to Jimmy Rollins and a single to Shane Victorino. With the tying runs on base and the dangerous Chase Utley at the plate, Rivera settled the threat with an inning-ending double play. In the ninth inning, Rivera worked around a Raul Ibanez double by striking out two Phillies, finishing off the Yankees' first World Series win.

The game was hardly a classic, but the Yankees felt satisfied, particularly with the way that Burnett pitched under the most pressurized of situations. In a span of three hours and 25 minutes, the Yankees had secured themselves a tidy 3-1 win, and a one-to-one deadlock in the World Series.

The Series now moved to Philadelphia and Citizens Bank Park, where the Phillies had dominated during the regular season. As rain poured down on a dreary Halloween night, the Phillies and Yankees waited out a delay of an hour and 20 minutes.

Once the rains abated, the pitching matchup in Game Three provided a deep contrast. The graying Andy Pettitte, one of four present Yankees with multiple World Series rings to his credit, took the ball for the pivotal third game. He faced the youthful Cole Hamels, a supremely talented left-hander who had muddled through a disappointing season.

For the first few innings, youth won out over age. The Phillies touched Pettitte for three runs in the bottom of the second, as the game took on the feel of one of those "Bad Andy" games that had popped up from time to time during the left-hander's postseason career. In the meantime, Hamels breezed through the first three innings as he looked every bit like the Phillies' ace he had been in 2008.

Then came the fourth inning, when the tide turned completely, and another bizarre and controversial play entered the annals of World Series play. It was another moment that became so critical to the Yankees' fortunes that October. With Mark Teixeira aboard on a walk, Alex Rodriguez lifted a deep fly ball down the right field line, where the ball appeared to strike a television camera and bounced back into the field of play. Rodriguez trotted into second base, completing what appeared to be a ground rule double.

Yet, there were questions. Was the TV camera in play or out of play? Should Rodriguez's drive be ruled a double or a home run? For the first time in World Series history, the umpires used instant replay to examine the call. Four of the six umpires went under the stands to watch the replay, conferred among themselves, and then returned to the playing field with a verdict. The ruling? The ball had hit the camera, which was considered beyond the field of play according to the pregame ground rules. A-Rod's drive was indeed a home run, giving the Yankees two critical runs and giving the Phillies reason to complain.

In the fifth inning, a rattled Hamels came completely unglued, as he gave up an RBI single to Pettitte, an American League pitcher who rarely came to the plate. Johnny Damon capped off the three-run rally with a two-run double, as the Yankees knocked Hamels from the game. The Yankees had turned a 3-0 deficit into a 5-3 lead halfway through the game. Hamels, who had looked so sharp in spinning shutout ball over the first three innings, had failed to last even five full frames.

In the sixth, the Yankees added another run as Nick Swisher homered against young left-hander J.A. Happ, before the Phillies responded with their fourth run against Pettitte in the bottom half of the inning. Back within two, the Phillies seemed to have life. Yet, the Yankees delivered a pair of knockout punches with single runs in the seventh and eighth innings, the latter scoring on a pinch-hit home run by Hideki Matsui, who had been reduced to backup status because of the lack of a DH in the National League's home park.

With a four-run lead and a deep bullpen, the Yankees held Game Three well in hand. Lefty specialist Damaso Marte retired the three batters he faced, and after a momentary lapse by Phil Hughes, Mariano Rivera came on to retire the final two batters of the night.

What had started out as a 3-0 deficit for the Yankees had transformed into an 8-5 win on the road. Not only had the Yankees changed the momentum within the game, but they had also altered momentum for the Series. Now owning a lead of two games to one, the Yankees could turn to staff anchor CC Sabathia in Game Four. This game would provide the defining moment of the entire 2009 postseason.

Unlike the Game One matchup, Sabathia would face journeyman right-hander Joe Blanton, and not Cliff Lee. Phillies skipper Charlie Manuel refused to use Lee on three days' rest, in part because Lee preferred pitching with a full complement of four days off. Though the Yankees had the clear advantage in the pitching matchup, Sabathia was not up to his usual caliber. The Yankees scored first, nicking Blanton for two runs in the top of the first. On some nights, two runs would have been sufficient for Sabathia, but the large left-hander lacked his usual control. The Phillies responded immediately in the bottom half of the first, scoring a single run before tying the game with another safety in the fourth.

In the top of the fifth, the Yankees opened up a 4-2 lead on RBI singles by Derek Jeter and Johnny Damon. But the Phillies did not collapse. In the bottom of the seventh, Chase Utley launched his third home run of the Series (all against Sabathia), his latest solo shot drawing the Phils within one. Having battled his control throughout the game, and with his pitch count at 107, Sabathia had gone far enough. Girardi handed the ball to Damaso Marte, who had suddenly become a reliable reliever after a spotty regular season. As he had done throughout the postseason, Marte retired the one left-handed batter that he was assigned, in this case the dangerous Ryan Howard.

As the game moved to the bottom of the eighth, Girardi turned to his primary setup man, Joba Chamberlain. The powerful right-hander retired the first two batters, before being shocked by journeyman third baseman Pedro Feliz, who rocketed a 96 mile-per-hour, full-count fastball into the left field stands. With one big swing, the Phillies had tied the game at 4-4, and now threatened to tie the Series.

Ruiz' home run set up a critical ninth. Phillies closer Brad Lidge retired the first two Yankees with ease. Lidge then came within a hair of striking out Damon, but the veteran outfielder managed to foul tip a ball that barely eluded the grasp of catcher Carlos Ruiz. Damon battled Lidge for nine pitches, the count running full, before he finally dumped an outside fastball into short left field for a single. With two outs, Damon knew that he needed to attempt a steal of second base to put himself in scoring position. He took off on the first pitch, decisively beating Ruiz's throw, which bounced on the infield grass. After sliding into second, Damon immediately popped up, and began racing toward third. Yankee fans watching at home must have wondered if Damon had lost his mind. Had the ball gotten away from third baseman Pedro Feliz, who was covering on the play?

No, the ball had not gotten away, and Damon had not lost his mind. Quite the opposite, Damon alertly realized that, with the Phillies employing a severe shift against Mark Teixeira, they were leaving third base unattended. That's why Feliz was covering at second base on the play, rather than one of the middle infielders. With Damon leaning toward third and Feliz lurching to the right of second base to field the throw, the 35-year-old left fielder knew that he could easily beat Feliz to third base.

With Damon now at third, Lidge was more reluctant

to use his best pitch, a diving slider that tended to bounce in the dirt. Not wanting to chance a wild pitch, Lidge stuck with his fastball and hit Teixeira with a pitch. With runners on first and third, up came Alex Rodriguez. Still hesitant to use his devastating slider, Lidge threw an inside fastball that A-Rod turned on quickly, pulling it hard down the left field line. The clutch double scored Damon, putting the Yankees in the lead at 5-4. Jorge Posada, who along with Jeter, Andy Pettitte, and Mariano Rivera represented the Yankee "Core Four," followed with a two-run single, sealing a magnificent 7-4 Yankee victory.

Damon's unconventional double steal—two stolen bases on only one pitch—represented the pinnacle moment of the Series. "You know how people always tell you that they've been in baseball for 40 years, 50 years, and things happen every game that they never saw [before]?" Yankees bench coach Tony Pena told ESPN.com. "Well, I've never seen that before. I never saw that before in my life."

The same could be said of most of the other coaches, managers, players, and fans in attendance at Citizens Bank Park. While Damon rightly received credit for a brilliantly heady play, Phillies shortstop Jimmy Rollins graciously took the blame for the Phillies' failure to cover third. Rollins told reporters that, as the captain of the infield, it was his job to signal to Lidge that he needed to cover third on any stolen base attempt. Rollins did not signal, and Lidge did not cover. And the Yankees now led the Series, three games to one.

With the Yankees in command, Game Five set up as somewhat of a concession game for New York. The Yankees would send A.J. Burnett, pitching on three days' rest, to the mound against Cliff Lee, the Phillies' ace who would work on his normal four-day interval. Even the most optimistic of Yankee fans could have been excused for expecting that the Series would return to New York for a sixth game.

The early returns favored the Yankees, but only briefly.

Mark Teixeira's first inning double scored Johnny Damon, giving the Yankees a 1-0 lead. Burnett, however, could not enjoy the prosperity. In the bottom of the first, the veteran right-hander allowed a leadoff single to Jimmy Rollins and then hit Shane Victorino with an errant pitch. That brought Chase Utley, the Phillies' most productive hitter of the World Series, to the plate. Jumping on a first pitch fastball, Utley ripped a three-run shot into the right field stands, shaking an uncertain Burnett. Lacking the command of his curveball, Burnett would allow three more runs in the bottom of the third, before departing with no one out and giving way to young right-hander David Robertson.

Staked to an early 6-1 lead, Lee did not pitch nearly as brilliantly as he had in Game One, but he pitched well enough. Over the first seven innings, Lee held the Yankees to two runs, as he protected an 8-2 lead, which was buttressed by Utley's second home run of the game and a solo shot by Raul Ibanez.

The Yankees finally erupted against a tiring Lee in the eighth. Alex Rodriguez, erasing all talk of his lack of clutch hitting in previous postseasons, scored two runs with a double, then came home himself on a sacrifice fly, as the Yankees chased Lee from the game. Drawing within three runs, the Yankees gave themselves a puncher's chance as they headed to the ninth.

Surprising some of the Philadelphia media, Phillies manager Charlie Manuel bypassed the slumping Brad Lidge, instead calling on set-up man Ryan "Mad Dog" Madson to close the game. The Yankees plated one run against Madson and brought the potential tying run to the plate on two different occasions against the interim closer, but they could draw no closer. With Damon on second base and Mark Teixeira at the plate, Madson struck out the switch-hitting power hitter to end the game. An 8-6 win gave the Phillies life, while pushing the World Series back to the Bronx.

If not for Utley, the Phillies' season might have already come to an end. With five home runs, the slugging second baseman had tied former Yankee Reggie Jackson for the most home runs in a single World Series. Unfortunately for the Phillies, Utley had not received enough support from the hitters in front of him; four of Utley's five home runs had come with no one on base.

Outside of Utley, most of the Phillies' big hitters had been calmed by Yankee pitching. With his rotation set exactly the way he wanted it, Joe Girardi had Andy Pettitte ready to pitch Game Six and CC Sabathia available for a possible Game Seven. The Phillies countered with Pedro Martinez, who had been mediocre in the second game of the Series.

Martinez was less than mediocre in Game Six. In the bottom of the second, Martinez issued a leadoff walk to Alex Rodriguez. He now faced Hideki Matsui, who was back in the lineup as a DH after being rendered a spectator for most of the three games in Philadelphia. Martinez tried to fend off Matsui with inside fastballs. "Making contact, some of them I fouled off," Matsui told reporters through his interpreter, Roger Kahlon, "but basically I was behind in the count. So I was in a tough situation. But fortunately there was one pitch that he threw that caught the plate, pretty much in the middle, so I was able to put a good swing on it, and so it was a home run."

Matsui's two-run drive gave the Yankees an early lead. That 2-0 advantage seemed like it might be enough with Pettitte on the mound, but the Phillies responded immediately with a run of their own in the top of the third, courtesy of Jimmy Rollins's sacrifice fly. The Yankees then went back to work in the bottom half of the inning. Derek Jeter's single, a walk to Damon (who later left the game after hurting his leg), and a hit-by-pitch of Mark Teixeira loaded the bases. Martinez caught Rodriguez looking for the second out. Up came Matsui. This time he laced a line single to center, scoring Jeter and Damon.

The Yankees added to their 4-1 lead in the fifth, as Chad Durbin took over for a fading Martinez. Jeter led off with a double, moved to third on a sacrifice bunt, and scored on Teixeira's single. Rodriguez followed with a walk. And up came that man again. This time, Matsui drove a fly ball deep to right against J.A. Happ, the ball eluding Jayson Werth for a double, which scored two more runs. The Yankees now led, 7-1, with six of the runs driven home by Matsui, whose early season slump and slowing bat speed had prompted some scouts to consider him over-the-hill.

To their credit, the Phillies showed some life in the top of the sixth. Ryan Howard's two-run home run made it 7-3. A double by Raul Ibanez pushed a tiring Pettitte to the dugout.

Joba Chamberlain finished the sixth without further incident, but ran into trouble in the seventh. Carlos Ruiz singled and Shane Victorino walked, bringing the dangerous Utley to the plate with two out. Girardi countered with Damaso Marte, who continued his magical postseason run with a swinging strikeout. The threat was over.

Marte started the eighth with another strikeout, this time against Howard. Even though Girardi still had a four-run lead, he took no chances the rest of the way. With one out in the eighth, he turned the ball over to Mariano Rivera, who worked around a double by recording a strikeout and a pop-up.

The primary suspense involved Rivera's pitch count. Would he be able to notch the final three outs without overtaxing his right arm, a situation that might force Girardi to summon another reliever? Rivera needed outs, but he needed them with some degree of economy. After a one-out walk to Carlos Ruiz, Rivera retired Jimmy Rollins on a fly ball. Rivera now faced Shane Victorino. On Rivera's 41st pitch of the night, Victorino bounced a slow roller toward the right side, where Robinson Cano fielded the grounder on the run and tossed to Teixeira for the final out. With a 7-3 win, coming on the night of November 4, exactly one week after an embarrassing blowout loss in Game One, the Yankees had claimed their 27ᵗʰ world championship.

Matsui's six-RBI night earned him Most Valuable Player honors for the Series. Pettitte, for the third consecutive postseason series, had won the clinching game, first against the Twins, then the Angels, and now the powerhouse Phillies. Additionally, Alex Rodriguez had won his first world championship, hitting .365 with six home runs throughout the postseason run, while turning back allegations of being some kind of postseason "choker."

After the game, Joe Girardi attempted to put the world championship, the Yankees' first since 2000, the fourth of Girardi's career, and the fifth for Jeter, Pettitte, and Rivera, in larger perspective. "Well, this is what the Steinbrenner family has strived for year after year, and has tried to deliver to the city of New York," said Girardi. "George Steinbrenner and his family are champions. To be able to deliver this to 'The Boss,' [in] the stadium that he created and the atmosphere he has created around here, is very gratifying for all of us."

As it turned out, it would be the last world championship for Steinbrenner. At one time the game's most dynamic owner, Steinbrenner would succumb to a heart attack during the summer of 2010. In his 37 years as the Yankees' principal owner, Steinbrenner watched his Yankees win seven world titles.

For those Yankee fans who remembered Steinbrenner's first two championship teams, the clubs of 1977 and '78, the World Series title of 2009 felt just as satisfying.

Acknowledgments

In recording more than sixty years of World Series memories, I returned to my own memory banks, record books, and scribbled-in notebooks. I also received immeasurable help from the recorded history of so many other sports journalists—from the Old Guard, many of whom I first knew some six decades ago, to the ambitious scribblers of today's press box crowds. I want to thank all of them for their marvelous reporting and I want to thank all the aging players of World Series games past for their contributions to this work. We all know in our advancing years how hard it is to find your keys or discover your glasses; but we also know how accurately and emotionally these heroes of long ago can stilll recite minute details of past events. I thank all of them for their kindness and their contributions.

Of course, I want to thank all the dedicated, hard working people at Sports Publishing for their efforts on my behalf, especially the intelligent, accurate, concise editing of Doug Hoepker. No book is the result of the efforts of a single person. This is a World Series winner thanks to all the members of this team contributing mightily.

Also by Maury Allen

Brooklyn Remembered: The 1955 Days of the Dodgers
Yankees: Where Have You Gone?
The Incredible Mets
Our Mickey (with Bill Liederman)
Joe Namath's Sportin' Life
All Roads Lead to October
Reprieve from Hell
China Spy
The Great Moments in Sports
Jackie Robinson: A Life Remembered
The Record Breakers
Memories of the Mick
Ron Guidry: Louisiana Lightning
After the Miracle
Jim Rice: Power Hitter
Roger Maris: A Man for All Seasons
Greatest Pro Quarterbacks
Sweet Lou (with Lou Piniella)
Baseball's 100
Mr. October: The Reggie Jackson Story
Damn Yankee: The Billy Martin Story
You Could Look It Up
Where Have You Gone, Joe DiMaggio?
Big-Time Baseball
Baseball: The Lives Behind the Seams
Bo: Pitching and Wooing
Voices of Sport
Now Wait a Minute, Casey
Reggie Jackson: The Three Million Dollar Man